John Macdonell

The land question

With particular reference to England and Scotland

John Macdonell

The land question
With particular reference to England and Scotland

ISBN/EAN: 9783743349612

Manufactured in Europe, USA, Canada, Australia, Japa

Cover: Foto ©ninafisch / pixelio.de

Manufactured and distributed by brebook publishing software (www.brebook.com)

John Macdonell

The land question

THE

LAND QUESTION

THE

LAND QUESTION

WITH PARTICULAR REFERENCE TO

ENGLAND AND SCOTLAND

BY

JOHN MACDONELL

BARRISTER-AT-LAW

London

MACMILLAN AND CO.

1873

LONDON : PRINTED BY
SPOTTISWOODE AND CO., NEW-STREET SQUARE
AND PARLIAMENT STREET

PREFACE.

I HAVE OMITTED all reference to the Game Laws and many other portions of the Land Question. Perhaps, however, the chief principles with respect to it have been stated; and the application of them is easy.

I must acknowledge my obligations for not a few practical suggestions to Mr. Webster, land surveyor, and to Miss McCombie, both of Aberdeenshire, who have aided me by information freely communicated, if indifferently utilised.

J. M.

March 10, 1873.

CONTENTS.

CHAPTER   PAGE

I. THE SUBJECT 1

II. FREE TRADE IN LAND 8

III. THE PRINCIPLES OF THE QUESTION . . 44

IV. URBAN LAND 83

V. AGRICULTURAL LAND 108

VI. PROPERTY IN MINES 174

VII. COMMONS AND WASTE LANDS 206

APPENDIX A. 251

LAND QUESTION

CHAPTER I.

THE SUBJECT.

ALL men love land, and the land question comes home to all. People are disposed, as perhaps they never were before, to scrutinise and question the policy and character of the laws specially governing the use and distribution of the soil of England. From men of almost all shades of political colour come words of doubt or open censure with respect to this portion of our law. 'Back to the land,' say not a few of the common people : they are irritated at the spectacle of the great bulk of the soil of England being owned by some thousands

B

of persons;[1] they will not believe that this aggregation of property in few hands was brought about and is maintained by natural and legitimate causes. 'Back, therefore, to the land,' say those people, filled with a dim, perhaps an unhistorical, idea that it was once theirs, and buoyed up by a hope— perhaps false also—that in some way or other they will yet share in the ownership of the soil. We may be told that such fantasies are the staple dreams of democrats of all time—the current coin of those who, jealous of their social superiors, are wounded by the very sight of all that they do not enjoy, and who make principles of their dislikes. But it is a new thing, and one of much significance —distinguishing the present movement from the abortive agitation of Fergus O'Connor for land reform—that thoughtful men and good citizens see much to be amended in the land laws, and that

---

[1] It is true that the returns obtained with a view to illustrate the probable results of Mr. Gladstone's Reform Bill of 1866, show the number of male freeholders to have been 358,526. But it can be alleged that there are as many landowners, only in the same sense that it is geographically true to say that there are thirty millions of Christians in the United Kingdom.

not a few economists and jurists are found avowing that they sympathise with much of the often blind demands of the poor. Never, and in regard to no other question, has there been a closer and quicker communication between the thinker and the workman. A novelty, indeed, witnessed in regard to no other political question, has been the power of the uneducated classes to take in swiftly, and to understand, somewhat abstruse or abstract economical theories relating to land. From the lips of the very class which owns it, I might gather materials for the framing of the indictment of the existing system — professions of generosity in admirable contrast to the law; confessions of defects therein; prompt disavowals of an intention to avail oneself of it to the full extent; and proofs of a thousand kinds that the landowners are, in practice, better than the laws which have been made so often for their advantage.

I mention only one such testimony. It is, perhaps, enough. Lord Derby has sneeringly alluded to the multitude of 'land quacks' now abroad; and he has thereby borne witness to the existence of

serious defects in the land laws which he extols ; for
quacks live by the presence of disease, and flourish
by the presence of pestilence.[1]

Now, to examine dispassionately the seething
mass of suggestions scattered about, and to sift the
truth from a heap of writings and talk, forms the
task of those who would investigate the land question—a question which begins to overshadow all
other political problems set before the country;
one, perhaps, of that rare kind which, with no
rhetorical flourish, we may say that States must,
in good time and in a wise fashion, solve or
decay. It is not, I repeat, rhetoric to say so. A
people are what their land system makes them ; the
soil that they till is stronger than they ; and the
essence of their history records the changes in the
ownership of their land. Frugal and industrious,
or unfixed and unstable in their ways, they are
according to the nature of their tenure of land ; and,
saving the birth of a new religion, or the influx of

[1] We were lately told that already the land agitation had,
in some instances—particularly in Ireland—affected prices and
the terms of mortgages. See *Law Times*, December 25, 1869,
and January 8, 1870.

a new race, or the lapse of time itself, there is, perhaps, no force more subtilely potent over a nation than the character of its land laws. Disappointingly feeble as is most political machinery to alter men for better or worse, and apt as is most legislation not in accordance with the current of society, to glance off the cuirass of ancient prejudices and adverse habits, a statesman has one instrument which pierces through all obstacles and uses men as clay. That instrument is legislation affecting land. A Stein or a Hardenberg, who knows how to use it, may shape the morals and destiny of a people. On the one hand, he may create a land system which will raise assassination into the likeness of a virtue, and make patriotism a byword, and frugality scarcely prudent; or he may scatter the seeds of hope among people that moiled and tilled with no thoughts beyond the horizon of to-day; he may inspire the humblest cotter with an affection towards his one field—somewhat sordid, perhaps, but deep as that which any member of an ancient family feels for his broad ancestral acres; and at the touch of wise land laws, even an

Ireland may grow into a happy country, the home of a contented people. Who has not marked the strangely swift decadence of an evicted family of old local standing, from industrious, frugal ways into shiftlessness, and in the end vice, and sometimes the ascension of an idler or vagabond to an outwardly well-ordered life, all by reason of his being put into some farm or little plot where he may labour with certainty of gain? and observing such moral transformations, who could not but feel how potent for good or for evil were the statesmen or legislatures that could determine which of those two highroads to vice or virtue a large part of any nation should pursue? Everyone's experience will tell him that few things exhaust men's immense capacity for misery more nearly than a bad land law. So much one may say without extolling this or that form of tenure as the best. National regeneration by spade husbandry is not here advocated, nor are there any covert allusions to the benefits of large farms and large estates. The partisans of both systems will agree in branding each other's nostrum as a canker or poison, and this circumstance is one of many testimonies to the vast influence of any form of land tenure. Now, on England, in particular, lies the duty of self-examination. If she be right, she is right alone. If she be wrong, she errs alone.

Of course, our subject may be so understood as to comprehend almost every topic connected with the tenure of land. The best modes of rotation, according to soil and climate, drainage, steam cultivation, and tillage, might be so many portions. But these and many other matters lying near the margin are excluded, and a subject at once well demarcated, large, and important is encompassed, when we select for examination the chief peculiarities of the laws affecting land, their defects, and the best practicable improvements.

CHAPTER II.

LET us, in the first place, turn to some defects
touching land of all sorts, agricultural and urban ;
let us then pass to the consideration of each variety.
I begin with what is a little infelicitously called
' Free Trade in Land.' I do so for many reasons.
To it Parliament has put its hand. The question
demands no preliminary study of the differences
between land and other kinds of property. With
' free trade,' according to many, would come all that
is needful.

Now, nominally the last obstacle to the free
alienation of the soil was destroyed in the reign of
Charles II., when the right to devise by will was
completely established.[1] In reality, however, not
a little of the soil of England is still *extra commer-*

[1] 12 Car. II. c. 24.

cium; a much larger portion of it cannot be easily
sold ; and if we mean by 'free trade in land' the
power of cheap and expeditious selling, it has yet
to be created. The existing obstacles are many,
a few of them real, no doubt, the majority artificial
and needless. The fact that this kind of property
is of permanent value, that complicated interests
surely gather about it, and that possession is no
strong evidence of complete ownership, makes it
necessary to inquire more minutely before one buys
land than before one buys a bale of goods. Each
acre has a history and a character of its own. We
cannot measure off so many roods like so many
yards of cloth. Fiscal duties stand in the way ; we
pay no duty on the occasion of the transfer of
Consols, but the State imposes a heavy tax in the
shape of stamp duties on the transfer of land. So
far there are genuine difficulties, perhaps not to be
removed. But we face a more substantial and less
defensible obstacle to the bringing of land into the
market, when we say that the destination of much
of England—perhaps of two-thirds, and certainly
not much less than one-half—was determined ten,

twenty, thirty, or even sixty years ago, and that it
will not be free sixty, thirty, twenty, or ten years to
come. The present inhabitants of a large area of
England own it only in the sense that they may do
with it as the past inhabitants, in their wisdom or,
it may be, their folly, deemed proper. What
portion former generations did not lock up, that we
may sell : they might have locked up the whole for
a time, for aught the law said to the contrary ; and
perhaps we ought to be more grateful than we are
that so much has been left at the disposal of this
age. This condition of property is commonly but
erroneously ascribed to the existence of entails.
And, no doubt, there was a time in the history of
England when estates were so entailed that the free
circulation of property in land was seriously im-
peded. After the passing of the statute De Donis
Conditionalibus in the reign of Edward I.,[1] the grasp
of ' the dead hand ' lay heavy on the soil. Previous
to the passing of that statute, sales or rather
subinfeudations had been common and easy. In
spite of the resistance of feudal superiors, anxious

[1] 13 Edw. I. c. 1.

to retain estates in the same families for the sake of their chance of the reversions, the strict letter of the grantor's deed of gift was disregarded. An estate had been given, let us suppose, to A and the heirs of his body; the moment a son was born to A, he was considered free to sell the estate and disappoint the grantor. Seeing their expectations thus undermined, the nobles resolved to make an effort to preserve their imperilled or waning rights over their tenants; and accordingly there was passed, at the instance of the interested barons, the famous 'De Donis Conditionalibus,' which declared that if a gift of 'tenements' or land were made to A and the heirs of his body, he might not sell or alienate them to a stranger, or anyone not heir of his body. Henceforth the heir was to take everything from the grantor, nothing from the grantee. Disastrous was the result of this attempt to establish perpetual entails,—so disastrous that the judges, not unwilling to weaken a law which was working incalculable mischief in the realm to debtors, parents, children, the Crown, and industry, winked at evasions of the statute, and

suffered it to be undermined by fictitious suits termed
common recoveries.   By-and-by Parliament permitted the use of fines.   Both recoveries and fines
were clumsy modes of breaking or barring entails.
Yet these processes, with their solemn falsehoods,
leading, as Bentham says, to 'the fabrication of
pickpocket and mendacious instruments,' were
employed until 1833.   Only then was the power
to bar an entail in a swift and rational manner
created by the 'Abolition of Fines and Recoveries
Act.'   He who would do so now needs not the aid of
Richard Roe or John Doe ; a short deed enrolled
in the Court of Chancery enables a tenant in tail in
possession to bar an entail.   It is true that there
is wont to be a protector to the settlement, and
that without his consent only a base fee or an
estate somewhat less than the fee simple can be
obtained.   But a tenant in tail in possession is usually
entirely uncontrolled.   With the exception of a few
estates, such as a small portion of the Marlborough
estates, given on account of public service to some
general and his descendants, there are in England no
instances of strict entails; and if there were no checks

on the free circulation of property, except such as
.are due to the permission to create estates tail, trivial
indeed would be the cause of complaint.

It is of settlements we complain. It is life
tenancies, not entails, which are the chief obstruc-
tion to 'free trade,' and the great bane. It is
the cunning of conveyancers rather than the errors
of the Legislature, which has fenced about so much
of the soil of England; for the law of settlements
and the kindred law of perpetuities are judge-made.
Nor are they of ancient origin. Mr. Joshua
Williams, Q.C., in an elaborate paper on the subject,
states that there is to be found before the 3 & 4
Philip and Mary no specimen of the present general
form of a marriage settlement; that is to say,
tenancies for life with remainders in tail to the first
and other sons.[1]

The power of barring, by recoveries and fines, an
entail, led to the employment of life tenancies, which
were inserted before the estate tail. But even this

[1] See Mr. Lewis' work on the manner in which the law of
perpetuities was constructed. I need scarcely say that the
necessity of protecting contingent remainders by means of
trusts has been removed by the 8 & 9 Vic., c. 106, s. 8.

precaution was liable to be defeated, owing to a technical rule relating to *merger*; and so the conveyancer, ever ready with new fetters when they were in demand, invented what were called ' trusts for preserving contingent remainders,' which prevented the life tenant from acquiring a larger estate and from selling. The judges had decided in Mary Portington's case that no tenant in tail could be deprived, even by special terms, of the right to bar the entail. But here was their work almost undone. In considering the type of the modern settlement, let us recollect that it does not express the deliberate resolution of the Legislature. No Parliament ever agreed that a man should grant tenancies for life to any successive number of persons in existence, to the whole human race if he likes, with a remainder over to some one unborn. Judges and the labours of a long series of lawyers, from Sir Orlando Bridgman, and including Palmer, Booth, Pigot, and Duval, have made or perfected those chains which enable a landowner to direct the destination of his property in circumstances which he does not know, to shape the fates of people whom he has never seen, and, generally, to rule in a world that is not like his own.

Settlements creating life tenancies, with remainder in tail, would be unendurable if men used to the full extent the power which they possess, and if Parliament had not repeatedly applied its correcting hand. A tenant for life has no strong motive to improve his estate. Why should he do so? His interest ends with his life. His improvements will enrich his successor, perhaps a stranger. And, then, it is the unfortunate fact that he acts as a lure to ensnare others. Sacrificed himself to the Moloch of family ambition, and a slave to the passion for territorial distinction, which generally recruits its most fanatical adherents among those whom it has undone, the father persuades his son, the remainder man, in return for an allowance during their joint lives, to disentail the estate, and re-execute a new settlement on his reaching the age of twenty-one. And thus, cycle after cycle, in many a family the process is repeated; there is a perpetuity in fact, if not in name. We have had in mind a very simple form of settlement, one much simpler than that

commonly employed. Generally desirous to reconcile justice to his wife, younger sons, and daughters,
with a thirst for family immortality, the settlor loads
his estate with charges, jointures, or portions; so that
it is probable that the tenant for life enters into
possession without capital or enough of it.[1]   Until
Parliament came to the rescue, how impotent for
good was the tenant for life!   He could not always
grant leases.   The presumption was, that he was
poor; and if he were not so, why should he sink his
own money, how could he persuade others to sink
theirs, in land which passed from his control at death?
Unable to sell, he could not reduce his estate to the
measure of his means.   Could his position be much
worse?   Some of those glaring evils were admitted
by the Legislature to be unendurable; and, while all
attempts to destroy life tenancies have been scouted,
there has been passed a series of Acts of Parliament which approximate the status of the tenant for
life to that of the owner of the fee simple.   The

---

[1] ‘La plupart de nos grands propriétaires gagneraient à pos-
séder moins de terre et plus d'argent.'—LÉONCE DE LAVERGNE,
Economie rurale de l'Angleterre, quoted by Mr. Fowler.

Settled Estates Act [1] authorises the Court of Chancery to grant power to permit leases and sales of settled estates when that can be done consistently with a due regard to the interests of all persons entitled under the settlement. The Court also received authority to permit sales of timber and to direct the laying out of estates as streets, roads, squares, or gardens. Lord Cranworth's Act of 1860 [2] was passed, as the preamble says, on account of the expediency of attaching to settlements certain powers which it is usual to insert therein, but which sometimes are omitted. It attached to every settlement a power of sale and exchange, unless the terms of the instrument expressly forbade it. In England various Improvement of Land Acts, and in Scotland the Montgomery, Aberdeen, and Rutherfurd Acts, not to speak of others less important, have been successively passed, with a view to emancipate the life tenant still further, and to make his position in some degree compatible with the performance of the duties of a landowner. [3] In passing these

[1] 19 & 20 Vic. c. 120.   [2] 23 & 24 Vic. c. 145.
The latest is the 33 & 34 Vic. c. 56, which empowers

Acts, Parliament did indeed bear witness to its
consciousness of the evils which flowed from strict
settlements.   But the remedies were inadequate;
the root of evil 'remained in the ground; and we
may doubt whether Mr. McCulloch was right in
affirming that 'in its present state the law of entail'—he speaks of settlements—' comes very near
perfection.'   The first of the English Acts which
we have mentioned can generally be brought into
operation by an applicant only when the assent of
the parties beneficially interested in the settlement
and of trustees is procured.   Then, too, the length
of leases which a tenant for life may give may
not be sufficient for a tenant desirous to improve
and drain wet land with no good fall, and anxious
to protect himself against liability to bad seasons.
And as to the Act which allows of sales by trustees,
its effects are blunted by the necessity of reinvest-
ing the proceeds in land.   The aggregate quantity
of land for sale is not increased.   The acres are
shuffled, but not released.   It is true, too, that

limited landowners to charge their estates for the erection of
suitable mansion-houses.

Parliament has, by the private and public Drainage
Acts, permitted owners of settled estates to lay out
their own or Government money for purposes of
improvement, and to make such debts preferential
charges on their estates. But the conditions on
which the loans are granted do not always suit a life
tenant. 'Montgomery improvements' have been
in Scotland fruitful sources of difficulty.

It is a curious commentary on the absence of a
directing intelligence in legislation, that Parliament
was at one and the same time engaged in repelling
direct attacks on settlements and destroying their
efficacy. Such enactments, tending to invest the
tenant for life with the powers of the owner of the
fee simple, seem, however, to be so many steps towards an enactment which shall convert the former
into the latter.

It is often said that the charges against settlements are pure chimeras or exaggerations, since
every well-drawn deed contains powers of sale and
leasing.[1] That, however, is not quite correct; a

[1] *Free Trade in Land.* By William Hayes, Barrister-at-
Law.

settlement would never be made if it were true, and
the sole circumstance which gives it the colour of
truth is, that within limits it is customary to invest
the tenant for life with some discretionary power.
Yet, in fact, a modern settlement is in some respects
more tyrannical than those of the old type. 'The
tendency of the present generation of conveyancers,'
says Mr. Davidson, 'is, on the one hand, to shorten
assurances by abridging recitals, omitting synonyms
and useless expressions, and abbreviating language
generally ; and, on the other, to lengthen all instruments, except the simplest, by inserting powers and
clauses to meet numerous possible events which were
not contemplated in former times.' [1]

Now, is this longing to gratify far-stretching
ambition which invades the future, this wish for a
monument in the shape of many even if barren
acres and of pinched but not landless descendants,
or the death-bed certainty that one who cannot
know the facts is, with a lawyer at his elbow, the
best judge of the fitness of family arrangements for

---

[1] Davidson, *Precedents in Conveyancing.*

the next half-century, a hallowed feeling to be tenderly touched? I doubt it. It seems needless to go out of the way to satisfy those who would drink to the dregs their powers as landowners. A man's right to dispose of his own does not comprehend the right to dispose of the time of the courts and judges of the future, and to bind them to enforce, years after he is in dust, the arrangements which were planted by vanity—that vanity which, to quote Lord Chancellor Nottingham, 'fights against God, by affecting a stability which human providence can never attain to,' which may work towards the impoverishment of the soil, and which makes children from their cradles independent of their own exertions or their parent's love or esteem. This ugly tenacity to the goods of life, and this want of courage to believe that all will go well when a man dies, are rather poor things; and probably they would receive meet treatment, all conflicting interests would be reconciled, all just claims appreciatingly dealt with, if it were declared that 'no man ought to be allowed to regulate the succession to anyone

but himself.'[1] It is far from obvious what injustice would of necessity be done were the power
to create life tenancies annulled. Children might
still be provided for. It would still be possible to
leave independent those whom the death of a parent
or a husband would otherwise leave dependent.[2]

It may be interesting to examine the provisions
of the Code Civil on this head. The general
principle is: ' Substitutions are prohibited.' But in
two exceptional instances life tenancies are permitted. Book iii., title ii., c. vi. says that a testator
may give what portion of his property is disposable
by will to his brothers or sisters, subject to the
charge of transmitting the goods to the children born
and to be born, to the first degree only, of the said
brothers or sisters. The Code also allows fathers and
mothers to bestow a certain portion of their property
on one or several of their children, subject to the

---

[1] Lord Advocate Young, *Address to Law Amendment
Society*, November 30, 1870.

[2] The objection to strict settlements cannot be better put
than the following opinion of counsel as quoted in Mr. Hayes's
Introduction to Conveyancing, vol. i. p. 558: 'At best, such a
settlement is a speculation ; at worst, it is the occasion of
distress and profligacy and domestic discord.'

duty of restoring the property to their children born
and to be born. The Code declares that ·these dis-
positions will hold good only when the settlement is
for the benefit of all children without distinction of
age or sex. These regulations do not merit close
imitation; they aim at equality of property—a questionable benefit—and they do not wholly secure us
against land being controlled by ' a blind instrument '
instead of a living deeply interested intelligence. It
is observable also that the Code treats personal and
real property alike; and it has been contended by
many, that if we restrict the power of settlement
with respect to the latter, the principle of the Code
must be followed, and that we must do the same
with respect to the former also. Now, there is
personal property (a lease of 99 or 999 years, for
instance) possessed of all the essential incidents
of realty, and the grounds for objecting to the
settlement of land may be used against the settlement of long leasehold property; in logic and fact,
though rarely in law, they are classed together.
But I think that if we put them into one category
we shall have before us a species of property the

tying up of which is particularly objectionable and
prejudicial to the common weal. How far it is
proper to gratify family pride and presumptuous
confidence in one's foresight by the aid of law is a
problem which every settlement of property, per -
sonal or real, must moot; but, without here dis-
cussing all the great distinctions between land and
goods and chattels and shares, it is admissible to say
that on the surface there lies one clear demarcation
between land destined to produce wealth, the prime
source of revenue, the great capital of society, and
debenture bonds or bank stock, say, the ownership
of which merely determines how wealth actually
made shall be distributed. And I may add also that
a good deal of money actually settled is so with
reference to land; it is intended to be turned into
land which will be settled.

Of the soil of England we may say that nobody
knows who own it. Possession, a fair indication of
title to a horse or a piece of goods, does not assure
us that the estate of the possessor of Blackacre or
Whiteacre is not a life tenancy, that it is not encumbered with mortgages and subjected to annuities,

and that a remainder man will not come on the
field when the possessor dies. No complete, acces-
sible register of all these facts exists. They can
be discovered only after a protracted search in what
Cromwell termed ' a godless and tortuous jungle.'
Of *registered* charges affecting land there are sixteen kept in some half-dozen different places, and in
more than a dozen different books.[1] To ensure what
the Court of Chancery will regard as a marketable
title — not an absolute title — one must trace
every step in the history of the estate for the last
sixty years; and as the nominal and beneficial
owners are often different persons, it is necessary to
follow the history of both the legal and equitable
estates. A bought-and-sold note signed by a
broker, disposes of the ownership of a cargo of tea;
a transfer on the shipping register, with a statutory
declaration appended—an operation perhaps costing
5s.—or a substitution in a bank's books or in a
company's register, may suffice to change the ownership of the value of thousands of pounds. But when

[1] *Report of Royal Commission on Land Transfer Act*,
p. 113.

you purchase realty you must be prepared for delay, cost, and perplexity. An offer is made in the auction room on the strength of personal inspection, or of the conditions of sale and printed description. A deposit is paid; the vendor's solicitor sets to work to prepare an abstract of title, carrying his researches back as far as sixty years if there be no stipulation to the contrary; the purchaser's solicitor, aided by counsel it may be, goes over the same ground, and compares the abstract with the original documents; then come objections and requisitions; and before a title is made out, it may be necessary to carry the inquiry into many collateral matters, and six months may have elapsed before a conveyance is effected. When a second sale takes place, there is a repetition of this trouble and expenditure. When a mortgage is contracted, there is another search into the same facts. In short, to guard against the contingency of the concealment of a settlement investing some one with rights as remainder man, it is necessary, if a title such as the Court of Chancery will approve, be desiderated, and if there be no stipulation releasing the bargain from this condition,

that the search be conducted sixty years back; and
the same process must be repeated each time the
estate is disposed of. The cost of transferring land,
particularly when all of it is not held on the same
title, is consequently enormous. If the estate is
small, the costs may equal the purchase-money; [1]
and in order to spare themselves the cost of a sixty
years' search persons are often content to take a
twenty-five to thirty years' title. Much of this
secrecy concerning the transfer of land and transactions affecting it is of modern origin. The old
symbolic mode of conveyance imperfectly served an
end which is now best effected by a register. It was
necessary to give livery of seisin in order to convey
an estate. Openly, and in the presence of your
neighbours, you, the feudal vendor, gave to the
purchaser a clod or piece of turf taken from the

[1] In Menzies' *Scotch Conveyancing* will be found a curious
list of the symbols of seisin. For mills, ' clapper and hopper; '
for teinds, a sheaf of corn; for patronage, a psalm-book and
key of church; for houses, hasp and staple. Menzies mentions
that in the case of the *Town Council of Brechin* v. *Arbuthnot*,
the Court of Session held a seisin of land void 'because it did
not mention delivery of earth and stone, but of stone only.'
This was in 1840.

land you sold. It was the symbol that you publicly delivered to him the land.[1]

Now, livery of seisin, says Sheppard's 'Touchstone,' 'was first invented as an open and notorious act to this end, and that by this means the country might take notice how lands do pass from man to man and who is owner thereof, that such as have title thereunto may know against whom to bring their actions, and that others may know that have cause of whom to take leases, and of whom to require wardship.' There was, therefore, once an open mode of conveying freehold land; and the same may be said of copyhold land, which was, and is, openly transferred in the Customary Courts of Manors by surrender, as the process is termed.[2]

---

[1] Mr. Hughes, in his *Practice of Sale of Real Property*, vol. i. p. 6, mentions the case of an estate which was sold in 200 lots, and the vendor of which expended 2,000*l*. in furnishing the purchasers with attested copies of the title-deeds. One may here express an opinion that the forms of certain commercial instruments might with advantage be changed. An ordinary marine insurance policy or a charter-party is drawn with pious but embarrassing grotesqueness.

[2] It may, perhaps, be generally forgotten that Lord Brougham's solution of the question of the easy transfer of land was the application to freehold land of the mode used with respect to copyholds.

That a register should be established, and that it should be something better than what often is now its substitute, the valuation book, is a point on which almost all thoughtful men are agreed ; and though it is two hundred and twelve years since a committee of the House of Commons first gave their assent to the principle, the delay in creating an efficient system cannot last much longer.

We all know that the Act of 1862 has failed. Lord Westbury, its promoter, wished to effect two or three objects, one of which was to give indefeasibility of title to all landowners whose titles would bear scrutiny for sixty years back. This circumstance of itself was sufficient to damn the Act ; for purchasers generally, and mortgagees often, are content to take a title of thirty or forty years' standing, and the difference in value of an estate, owing to the possession of a Parliamentary title, does not recompense the cost of registration. The obstacles, too, in the way of registering any but indefeasible titles were a wilful sacrifice of possible benefits. Obviously, every system of registration should be readily open to imperfect titles, so that

they should ripen into perfect titles. In course
of time all titles would be perfected by this
process, recommended by at least two Royal
Commissions; and if it were made compulsory to
register on every occasion of sale, there would be
perfected, at no distant date, the titles of almost all
estates in England. The next desideratum seems
to be that there should be on the register an absolute owner for each parcel of land, and that all
conflicting interests should be guarded by a system
of notices. In this respect Lord Cairns's bills of
1859 come much nearer to what is wanted than
Lord Westbury's Act. The former proposed to
establish a Landed Estates Court similar to that
existing in Ireland. That Court was to be empowered to give to proprietors a title which should
be good against the world. As in the case of
stock or ships, there was to be one ownership registered, and other interests were to be protected
by caveats or inhibitions. To the principle that
there should be some person registered as absolute
owner, as in the case of stock, Lord Westbury and
Lord Selborne have objected that this would mean

the registration of 'a fictitious ownership,' and that it would be essential to make an arduous search into the caveats. But this objection does not seem quite conclusive. If a purchaser only knew that all the parties concerned were on the register, and that when the 'land stops,' and 'money stops,' to use the nomenclature of the Land Transfer Commission, were removed, the concurrence of all parties had been obtained, there would be no small gain. Perhaps we may say that, if the vendor made an unimpeachable title when he cleared the register, there would be an enormous saving of time and money. For what is wanted does not so much appear to be a perfect register of assurances such as exists in Scotland, or an imperfect register of assurances such as Lord Westbury established; at present, we chiefly want the register to give notice of all claims affecting land such as a personal inspection of it might not disclose, and all that may be accomplished by a judicious use of caveats, cautions, and stops. Leases, mortgages, sales—in short, the whole history of the estate—ought to be indicated, if not written in full, on the face of the

register.[1] A register of assurances may be advantageous; in the meantime, let us have a registry of titles.

It seems desirable also that the registers should
be local and, if I may use the term, self-contained.
Such is the character of the admirable registers of
Denmark and the Grand Duchy of Hesse, where, to
quote Mr. Morier, ' there is, as it were, a conveyancer's office established at every proprietor's door,
doing business according to a minimum scale of fees,
to express which in English coin we must have
ccourse to farthings.' Much of the benefits of
registration would be lost, particularly with reference to mortgaging, were the system centralised;
and it is a marked defect in some of the various
Government bills which have been introduced into

---

[1] The instances are rare in which settlements are con-
cealed, and yet, to guard against the possibility, the public
needlessly expend hundreds of thousands of pounds. It is
generally a too sure sign of sloth or defective civil law
when the criminal law must be intensified. Manufacturing a
misdemeanour is a lame substitute for a register such as almost
all countries but England have long possessed; and yet this
device has been employed by Parliament, which, while
declining to create an effective system of registration, has made
the concealment of any incumbrance or instrument material
to the title a misdemeanour.

Parliament, that they disregard the high advantage of localising the registers. Probably for London not one, but several would be needed. Lastly, if defeasible titles, as well as indefeasible, are freely allowed to be placed on the register, there seems to be no good reason why registration should not be made compulsory, at all events on sale, or within a certain period. It is not sellers or purchasers alone that are interested in the free circulation of property in land; it is the concern of the whole community. If we insist upon the registration of the ownership of all ships and of mortgages affecting them, notwithstanding the repeal of the 'Navigation Laws,' the original cause of the use of marine registration, *à fortiori* is it expedient in regard to land.[1]

Probably, however, if we desire to facilitate the sale of land very much, it will be necessary to do more than create a system of registration. It was the boast of Lord Westbury that his Act left the law of real property intact. That circumstance was rather a weakness than an excellence; and we shall

[1] Abbott on Merchant Shipping, 11th edit. p. 44.

never see land circulate with that freedom which is desirable if it is to be a ready instrument of commerce, unless the number of interests, which it is permissible to create, are diminished, and unless the period of prescription necessary to bar claims, is shortened. Stops and caveats on the register will be of great service as indicating the number of n - quiries to be made, and as a correct index of the interests concerned; perhaps they will not diminish the size and intricacy of the volume to which they are the index.[1] That must be done by legislation of a very delicate character. Let us look at the cases in which it might be proper and expedient to permit the creation of interests less than the fee simple. I do not now speak of short leases or those interests for which money would be an adequate equivalent,

---

[1] 'The question then is :—Are, or are you not willing to give up your plan of settlements ? '—Joshua Williams, Q.C. ' So long as the law permitted, as it did, greatly to the public advantage, a system of estates for life with remainder in tail, and portions for younger children, with other complicated arrangements, the House might continue to have glittering pictures of simplicity to titles, which would, however, last only for a time.'—Mr. (now Vice-Chancellor) Malins. *Hansard*, February 14, 1859.

but of those which ought to remain as interests
in land. Clearly infants and posthumous children
must be provided for. It might be fairly demanded
that there should be power to create estates ter-
minating on their attaining majority. Perhaps,
also, the capacity to give a life estate to one's widow
ought to remain. In such circumstances the land
might be locked up, and a *distringas* might prevent a fraudulent transfer. So far the cases in which
the proprietor naturally desires the fee simple of his
estate to go to some one, subject to a life or other
partial prior interest. But he may desire—and in
almost every settlement there is shown a desire—to
split up an estate into several portions, and to burthen it with certain charges—rent-charges, portions
for children, &c. Now, applying to his wishes the
rule that there should always be some one capable
of selling, I think that the proprietor might be called
upon to elect between converting all or part of his
land into money or giving to his heir the estate,
subject, indeed, to charges for certain persons, but
with the right to pay them off whenever the latter
pleased, and under a corresponding obligation to pay

them off whenever they gave due notice. Instead of
loading the land with permanent charges, it would be
expedient to make all such charges convertible into
money at the will of the owner or the persons in
whose favour they are made. Let there be a thousand money interests in land and but one interest of
ownership; let there be no life tenancies, unless,
indeed, the case of widows ought to be an exception;
let trustees protect the interests of those incapa-
citated by tender age or insanity; let other interests be convertible into money; let caveats on
the register indicate their existence; let property
pass by registration and let deeds be the authority
to register—such seems the path of reform. And
there is not, I believe, to be found in the many
and various precedents in Davidson's ' Conveyancing ' one legitimate object to which the conveyancer
lends his skill inconsistent with the changes here
suggested. Helpless children and widows would
be seen to. Families could still be founded. It
is, of course, true that any serious restriction on
the power of settlement might be inconvenient
were it not for the multiplication of safe channels

of investment. But while the public funds amount to nearly eight hundred millions, and the railway debenture stock of the United Kingdom to more than sixty-seven millions, there will probably be experienced no great inconvenience.

A good system of registration would, of course, increase the facility of borrowing. It would be unnecessary, as now, to transfer the fee simple to the mortgagee—a process almost rendered essential for safety so long as there is no register. A stop placed thereon would suffice to protect him. It has been proposed to enter all mortgages, as in the case of the register of ships. But that, at the outset, seems needless ; notices would suffice. No doubt, to be complete, it would be necessary to have registers of all interests not palpable ; but as a beginning a complete register of the ownership, with an apparatus of notices and stops, would probably suffice. In course of time we may hope to see subsidiary registers of all charges, of all leases of twenty-one years' duration and upwards, and, in fact, of all estates and interests not visible. Then would there be ' free trade,' not only in land, but in all interests therein. In order to make land a commodious article of commerce, there are needed other minor and auxiliary changes. A more rational and fair system of remunerating solicitors, so that it should be unnecessary to employ tautological forms, wherein ' feeble expletives their aid do lend,' to obtain the just reward of highly-skilled labour,[1] and the printing of all deeds bookwise, are two mechanical reforms of no mean consequence. I would also express a doubt whether the period of prescription might not, in the altered conditions of society, with facilities for communication so much increased, be shortened. It is a fair question whether, in guarding in every case against the contingency of being unfairly dispossessed, which scarcely ever occurs, we do not purchase immunity too dearly. The cases in which any moral claim would be frustrated by reducing the period to ten years, and to twenty in the event of there being disabilities, would probably be rare. The few instances in which railways

---

[1] ' You do not pay them properly for what they do, and you seek to make up for this by paying them for what they do not.' —Joshua Williams, Q.C.

taking land under parliamentary powers have had to pay compensation, seem to show this. Of course, with these reductions there would come a reduction of the period required by the Court of Chancery to be investigated before declaring a title 'marketable,' and such as a purchaser can be compelled to take. And here I would mention the expediency of all the effects of the deceased, whether they be land or not, passing into the hands of one official, executor or administrator, bound to administer them for the benefit of all creditors.[1]

Nothing has been said about the right of primogeniture, not because there is any desire to defend it, but because its abolition would not effect very much good. That the State should do in the case of intestacy what a man who makes his will rarely does—for the admirers of that right take care to leave their estates charged for the benefit of their younger sons and daughters—seems wrong. But were the right of primogeniture abolished, wills

---

[1] On this head, see the concluding chapter of Joshua Williams' *Essay on Real Assets*.

would still transmit the bulk of landed property to
eldest sons; and, indeed, while the present distinction between beneficial and equitable estates is
preserved, there would arise inconvenience in conveyancing from the abolition of the right of primogeniture.   Last, but not least in importance, among
reforms, would be the obliteration of the present
distinction in point of priority between crown and
judgment debts and ordinary debts.   If they ever
existed, sound reasons for the distinction are gone;
and with its disappearance would vanish all ground
for keeping the separate registers which are now
scattered about.   What a cause for satisfaction
when crown debts, judgments, *lites pendentes*, and
bankruptcies affecting an estate, shall be indicated
by notices or otherwise in one page of one book kept
at one office !

Most of the above arguments against settlements
are more or less applicable to the holding of land by
corporations not empowered to sell; and the un-
locking of the manacles of settlement would only
accomplish a small portion of the work which is
needful were all the existing trammels on the sale of

corporate property suffered to remain. Though it may not be always worse managed than private property which is settled, there is no security that it will be better managed than land which may be sold at any time ; and it seems mistaken policy to tie the hands of corporations, and prevent them from honestly disposing of their property. This error, it is submitted, is perpetrated by the ' Municipal Corporation Act,' which forbids the sale of land unless with the approbation of the Lords of the Treasury [1] ; and a like mistake pervades the arrangements with respect to not a few other corporations—for example, with respect to the University of Cambridge, the colleges of which are, indeed, permitted to sell their lands with the consent of the Church Estates Commissioners, but are compelled to devote the proceeds thereof to the purchase of other land.[2] In the officers of corporations, there is always a disposition to manage expensively, and not to sell ; and the legislator goes out of his way gratuitously and unnecessarily when he seeks to encourage this disposition. That public bodies

[1] 5 & 6 Wil. IV. c. 76, s. 94.   [2] 19 & 20 Vic. c. 88, s. 48.

should be compelled to sell their land when no
substantial charge of inefficiency against them has
been made good, seems superfluous ; but it is right
that they should be allowed to sell freely.   How far
the real abuses connected with corporate property
are due to inability to do so, is a question too rarely
asked and answered.   Let us condemn the management of public bodies only after they have received
the powers of private individuals.

Thus far have we gone without being obliged to
confront the revolutionary projects now rife for
alteration in the tenure of land.   So far, we do
little more than seek to make the law of realty the
same as, or similar to, that of personalty.   And here,
with many, ends the Land Question.   But here, to
my mind, the true problem only begins ; and those
who hope to appease discontent with plans, however
well devised, for making it easy to sell, and to buy,
and mortgage, and lease, will perhaps be signally
disappointed.   There may have been a time when
reforms such as have been here outlined would
have given peace.   Never naturally in England
do men favour thoroughgoing changes, or care

to alter the alphabet of our institutions. But the maintenance of minor abuses has more or less educated all classes in the knowledge of the principles of the subject, and they will apply them, be sure of it, to fundamentals as well as details. So to greater changes we must reconcile ourselves, sadly or joyously. Political discontent—oftentimes another name for the possession of an unsatisfied and lofty ideal of political excellence—will probably not be quenched by any bill yet draughted, or by legislation in accordance with any report yet adopted by a Royal Commission. The vast circumference of the hopes and plans now abroad compass much more than free trade in land.[1]

[1] See Appendix A.

CHAPTER III.

THE PRINCIPLES OF THE QUESTION.

DISCUSSIONS on revenue reform, or the best modes of devising 'ways and means' for the government of the country, are wont to be nothing but discussions on the merits of direct or indirect taxation. This ancient controversy, which moves, but does not advance, has submerged certain preliminary problems which it will be well to ventilate at this point. This is the first question : Is direct or indirect taxation always requisite for procuring a revenue ? The second question is : Does either of these form the ideally perfect mode of providing for the wants of governments? Is there another source from which they do not draw as they ought, and, if it exists, can it still be made to flow ? In answering these problems, we touch, it appears to me, the kernel of the Land Question, which

seems to be only a part of a still larger topic, and
which cannot be rightly discussed without the partial
consideration of a wider theme.   Such are a few
of the questions which, to a certainty, sometimes
come to one who meditates on the fiscal aspects of
politics, who seeks for light from the accredited
teachers thereof, and who is wearied and disappointed by this interminable battling round one, and
that not the chief, fiscal problems.   Such are the
questions which this chapter essays to answer in a
certain fashion—assuredly not in the hope of strik-
ing out some idea wholly new, and consequently
suspicious or self-condemned, but rather in the
belief that the answers to be submitted will appear
truisms which people never, or rarely, think of, and
axioms which they do not act upon.

Monopoly is a word coated with one knows not
how many ancient evil associations.   It recalls so
much of all that is wicked and foolish in the history
of our own country and that of others—the Tudor
monarchs throwing as largesses to their courtiers
offices and franchises which gave them the control
of the lives and property of subjects ; mischievous

trammels on industry, some of them loosened by the Statute of Monopolies, others remaining to trouble this generation; the trading privileges of the East Indian and Russian Companies; our colonial system with its foolish exclusiveness; the protection of our home industries—a long history of place-installed selfishness and error. And that name also brings up somewhat different, but also unpleasant, memories —the State trying to conduct trades for which it was essentially unsuited, and, in its desire to succeed, converting them into monopolies, to the grievous loss of the community; the State alone, for instance, growing or selling tobacco, and punishing all trespassers within its artificial domain. So disreputable and odious are the associations clustering round the word, that I hesitate to attach it to limitations of a very different character and altogether innocent. Monopolies they, indeed, all are; but some, if not all of them, are natural, spontaneous, and inevitable. They may be used well or ill, but monopolies they will remain. They do not arise out of the mandate of Parliament; and I may speak of them as natural monopolies. One class of them,

such as land and mines, are monopolies because
they, like other natural agents of production, are
limited.   They yield rent in the economist's meaning of the term.   Another class are less rigorously
of the nature of monopolies.   It is theoretically
possible that the tariffs of docks, canals, railways,
the post office, and the telegraph service, and the
rates of gas and water companies, should be regu-
lated by the fiercest competition.   For a time that
is sometimes the case.   But, in the long run, the
fact is not so.   ' Where combination is possible,'
said George Stephenson, ' competition is impossible ' ;
and in conformity to this principle, railway companies amalgamate, or ' divide the monopoly ; ' canals
fall into the hands of railways ; and gas companies,
ceasing to lay rival parallel mains, give up fighting,
and confine themselves, as in London, to different
districts.   Forbid open amalgamations, and sooner
or later there will be secret evasions in the form
of clandestine agreements to impose equal rates.
By-and-by the customer will discover that he has
not to deal with two vendors.   Such is the second
class of monopolies.   I take as the type of the third

class the issue of bank notes. It is generally believed, rightly or wrongly, that the emission of notes, if their convertibility is to be insured, ought not to be left to the discretion of private persons. It is the common notion that both the paper and the metallic currency should be under the control of the State. Notes payable on demand are, therefore, usually not left to the free action of supply and demand. In this, as in one and all of these monopolies, we witness the appearance of abnormal profits, and the existence of what may be called rent.[1]

---

[1] Perhaps here one may be allowed to advert to the loose and irregular way in which English statesmen have dealt with those natural monopolies. The State has taken over the postal and telegraph services. A promise has been given that the Irish railways will be purchased by Government if a reasonable price be charged. Our gas and water companies forfeit profits above 10 per cent. Our railway companies are bound by the maximum charge prescribed by Parliament, and are required under the Canal and Railway Traffic Act to furnish 'due facilities.' Oddly enough the natural monopolies, land and mines, the value of which depends so much on mere situation or some other accidental circumstance, and the banking monopolies created by the Acts of 1844 and 1845, are allowed to be enjoyed by private persons almost without check or hindrance. In the country districts of England we give to a few hundred banks, chosen according to no rational

With only one of these classes of monopolies have we here specially to do; but the above remarks help, perhaps, to show the true position of land. Economists have been at great pains to explain the nature of rent. Starting from the fact that the soil of a country is limited in extent, they have pointed out that even were it homogeneous, of uniform fertility, and equally commodious in all parts, the right to possess it would draw with it the power to exact rent as population expanded. The monopoly of a necessity of existence must create one kind of rent. Economists have also explained that, even if the soil of a country be practically unlimited, differences in fertility and situation will originate another kind of rent, that kind which Ricardo has called, not very happily, perhaps, the price paid for ' the original and indestructible powers of the soil.' We shall describe both kinds, if we speak of the one

rule, the authority to issue, for their own profit, notes to the value of some three million nine hundred thousand pounds; and in Scotland eleven companies, chosen owing to the mere accidental circumstance that they existed in 1845, have been invested with similar powers worth, directly and indirectly, thousands of pounds.

E

as rent originating in limitation of quantity, and of the other as rent due to differences in quality. We need not accept Ricardo's own account of rent as perfectly accurate. It may be true, as his critics have pointed out, that he substitutes cause for effect, when he ascribes the origin of rent to the necessity of resorting to a soil of greater poverty; that the growth of rent is really attributable not more to the enforced use of soils of lessening fertility than to the greater demand for certain parts of the soil actually cultivated; and that his theory oscillates between falsehood and unmeaningness. To Ricardo's theory it is often objected that much so-called rent, and in certain circumstances by far the most of what is called rent, is nothing but the return on capital and labour sunk in the soil. One could point to acres which ten years ago did not let for sixpence a-piece, and which now yield 10 per cent. on the outlay of their owner. The revenue drawn from a field once moss or heavy clay, but made worth 25s. an acre by drainage and deep ploughing, may be simply return on the capital. Another set of objections to Ricardo's account of rent arise out of the fact that there must be labour and capital expended somewhere before land is worth anything. I admit it; but the requisite expenditure need not be on the particular piece of land; the labour of landless people, say the making of a road or a railway, may give value to the property of the landowner. A third set of objections are drawn from the further fact that the return on landed property rarely exceeds three per cent. on the purchase money. That also is true, but not inconsistent with the above account; it only comes to saying that where no risk is run profits are small, or that a man may pay so much for getting the privilege of drawing surplus profit that his estate brings to him only the average, or less than the average, return on other investments of capital.[1] Be these objections right or wrong, it remains true that some land, if not all, differs economically from most

---

[1] There is, however, no denying the low rate of interest yielded by land. Though this is partially attributable to the perfection of the security, it is also due to other circumstances, one of which is that personal privileges are thrown as perquisites. While land is bought to fetch 3 to $3\frac{1}{2}$ per cent., land tax and rent charges of equal security are bought to pay 5 per cent. See Biden's *Rules for Valuers*. 10.

other kinds of property, and that it produces by
no corresponding labour or outlay of the owner
a surplus profit, which may be called 'economic
rent.' I cannot conceive the distinction between
land, or natural monopolies, and other kinds of
property being put more clearly and forcibly
than in the following passage which I take from
an essay by Professor Cairnes. 'A bale of cloth,
a machine, a house, owes its value to the labour
expended upon it, and belongs to the person who
expends or employs the labour : a piece of land
owes its value—so far as its value is affected
by the causes I am now considering—*not* to the
labour expended upon it, but to that expended
upon something else—to the labour expended in
making a railroad, or in building houses in an
adjacent town ; and the value thus added to the
land belongs, not to the persons who have made
the railway or built the houses, but to some one
who may not even be aware that these operations
are being carried on—nay, who perhaps has exerted
all his efforts to prevent their being carried on.'
Of the total proceeds of any acre of ordinary land,

so much is the return on the permanent or durable capital—drains, fences, &c.—invested therein; so much is the return on the circulating capital renewed annually, or at short intervals; and the residue is ascribable to permanent and inherent attributes of soil, situation, proximity to markets, roads, railways, &c., and to what I may term the general state of society. That the first part should accrue to the landowner if, as not unfrequently happens, he furnishes the capital for permanent improvements, is right; that the second should go to the usufructuary or farmer is also clear; and what seems equally indisputable is that the last, consisting of economical rent, should go to the general body of society. It having been shown that ' economical rent ' is paid for differences in quality and situation of land, created by no man, or that it originates in circumstances not to be credited to the landowner, it would naturally have been expected that from Ricardo's principles would have been unanimously and instantly deduced the conclusion that economical rent should not become the subject of private property, that no private individual should be permitted to monopolise 'the original and indestructible properties of the soil,' and what no man had created or earned by labour of his no man should own. It would have been only natural for all who accepted the preceding account of rent to hold that rent which proceeded from the common labours of the community should belong to it, that wages were not more fitly the reward of the labourer, or profits the reward of the capitalist, than was rent, as Ricardo understood it, the appanage of the community or State, and that, to quote the popular phrase, 'the land was the property of the people.' For these reasons, absolute property in land would appear to be theoretically unjust whenever economical rent appears. Of course, there might be cited other reasons why this should be so ; and, to name only one, land is a necessity of existence, and society might not subsist were men free to employ it as they pleased. We could not tolerate a race of proprietors of the stamp of the notorious Lucas, who wished to let his fields run to waste. We should be sacrificing the end to the means were we to suffer the landowner's rights to make the existence of society impossible, uncertain, or difficult. But one sufficient reason for denying absolute property in land, springs from the fact that its proprietor becomes, in the natural course of things, the recipient of an unearned residuum.

We shall, perhaps, be told that there is a great objection in principle to the conclusion here arrived at : it would bring the State into a region from which it should be excluded. Now, *laissez faire* is a good rule when the meddler is antagonistic to the meddled with ; but he seems to violate *laissez faire* most deeply who lets value which the community, or assuredly no single individual, has created be taken from it by private persons. And if it be possible for the State, or for municipalities, to manage any or all of these monopolies, there seems little standing in the way of the assertion that they are the primary resources of Government. Since there are many things from which their owners may, with ordinary exertion or no exertion at all, draw rent, or something above the usual profits on capital, if too much has not been

expended in the purchase, and since the State, ever
needy, is compelled at present to draw its revenue
from taxes which are a hardship to all, and a
grievous burthen to the poor, it is no paradox to
affirm that the maintenance of the State should be
provided, as far as may be, out of those funds
which Nature herself seems to have appropriated
to public purposes, arising as they do out of common or public exertions. The *onus* of proving
the expediency of letting even one of those funds
fall into the private domain rests on those who
propose it.   In one point of view, it matters little
perhaps whether the public or private persons own
the sites of cities.   But if one mode of tenure
brings vast wealth or competence to a few, and
releases so many from the wholesome bondage of
labour, and if the other relieves the whole community from burthensome taxes or rates, and eases
all a little without giving idleness to any, need we
hesitate or doubt as to which is preferable ?   Such
being the alternatives, do we not squander or pawn
the natural and primary resources of the State when
we suffer private hands to monopolise them ?   That

which presses on no man yet benefits all, is on the face of it a better mode of obtaining a revenue than that which mulcts all, it may be, unequally, and perhaps to the grievous injury of some. That which, taking from no man's just earnings, yet provides for the just common wants, is conspicuously superior to a system of which the true principle, according to Mr. Lowe, is that you must pinch every class until it cries out. An offer is made of a mode of raising revenue, which takes from none what they have rightly earned, which need rob no man of what he has rightly bought, and which will replenish the Treasury, no man being mulcted, no man wronged; and are we to reject this offer, and for ever allow so many private interests to gather round this public domain that it shall be useless and perverted? To a like question the answer once made was decidedly negative. For a time the revenue of this, as of every other State of Europe, came from rent. But the answer was revoked: the feudal duties incident to property fell into desuetude, and ultimately they were abolished; much of the Crown land was squandered; and for centuries the

nation has been reaping the harvest of its errors, each
sheaf whereof has been some tax, often vexatious and
cruel.   Ministers cannot govern the country for less
than 70,000,000*l*.   We vex the poor with indirect
taxes, we squeeze the rich, we ransack heaven and
earth to find some new impost palatable or toler-
able, and all the time, these hardships going on,
neglected or misapplied, there have lain at our feet
a multitude of resources ample enough for all just
common wants, growing as they grow, and so
marked out that one may say they form Nature's
budget.   Such seems the rationale of the subject of
which the land question forms a part.   And so we
may say that, if property in land be ever placed on a
theoretically perfect basis, no private individual will
be the recipient of economical rent.   Bastiat, it
may be mentioned, saw that logic and justice demanded no less ; and anxious to escape from such a
conclusion, and to buttress the fabric of society as
he found it, he sought to undermine Ricardo's
theory, and to prove, in the face of familiar facts,
that all rent was the return on the landowner's
capital.   Less logical economists in · this country

have at once expounded Ricardo's theory, and defended the position of the English landowner. How few have seen and owned the simple truth which follows from his doctrine is somewhat amazing, and equally strange is the small number of those who, having seen the truth, were courageous enough to utter it. Though the French physiocrats mixed their speculations on this subject with much dubious and even manifestly erroneous matter, to them belongs the merit of first directing attention to the propriety of drawing the revenue of the State from economical rent, or the *produit net* of Quesnay. Turgot, one of that school, says, ' the farmer has made this calculation (as to his outlay and remuneration); it is the surplus given to the landowner that forms revenue, and it is only on this that taxation ought to fall.'[1] The error of Turgot and the physiocrats was maintaining paradoxically that the State could, and ought to, touch this species of revenue alone, that they would not allow that several branches of industry also yielded a revenue

---

[1] ' Plan d'un Mémoire sur les Impositions.' Œuvres de M. Turgot, tome iv. p. 220.

which might be as fairly taxed or absorbed as the rent of the soil, and that rent betokened no peculiar virtue in land.

Waiving, at present, the numerous practical difficulties in the way of the realisation of the above principles in all their fulness, let us consider a few of the consequences which come to pass if the above be the true and ideal mode of raising a revenue. It follows that Adam Smith's famous canons of taxation, though excellent rules, to which all taxes should conform, are rules framed for somewhat abnormal times and circumstances, the canons, to put it strongly, of financial desperation, the maxims for the guidance of those who would follow not the best, but the next best course. Direct and indirect taxes imposed and collected according to those admirable rules may be necessary—so may loans. We know that at present the former are necessary—so, too, in certain circumstances are the latter. But, granting the above to be the ideal mode of obtaining revenue, it would follow, that just as we should seek to replace loans by taxes, so should we seek to substitute for the latter rent drawn from natural monopolies; and it would seem not unreasonable to hope, that as loans have ceased to be the regular resources of all solvent governments, so may taxes. Thus only shall we have the benefits of government without the burthens.

It follows, in the second place, that the fiscal system of England, far from being the best in existence, as is fondly assumed by those who know no other, is in reality one of the worst. Most other States have kept hold of some of these natural monopolies. Prussia draws not a little from monopolies.[1] At the end of this century France will be heir to railway property more than sufficient to cover the German indemnity. So far she has been wiser than we. In Belgium M. Rogier had the courage and wisdom to do with respect to railways what Sir Robert Peel and Mr. Gladstone failed to do. In Germany and France the canals are in the hands of the government. India annually raises

[1] ' As to the relative financial position of Prussia, the first noteworthy fact is, that she alone of the great States needs only to levy in taxation a little more than one-half of her nominal expenditure.'—Mr. Harris Gastrell's *Report on the Tenure of Land in Prussia.* 220.

some sixteen millions by the State being the land-owner; and but for this fact, our expensive form of government would be an impossibility in that poor country. It is we, in particular, who have suffered these primary resources to slip through our fingers. Or if there be one State which is showing as much folly as we have at divers times shown, it is America, which, undeterred by our example, is now flinging to the winds its splendid patrimony, and recklessly selling and allotting to railway companies or land jobbers what might be the national revenues of the future. What repentance awaits that country for having given to some of the former, grants of 25,600 acres per mile of road, and for assigning to the Northern Pacific Railway Company alone, 58,000,000 acres! [1]

And, granting the above theory to be true, does there not arise a conception of a beautiful, simple, and useful law, providing for the expenditure of the State, without the aid of statesmen's ingenuity, and with all the certainty of a physical law? We recognise the possibility of the normal revenue con-

[1] *Our Land.* By Henry George. San Francisco.

stantly keeping pace with the normal expenditure. Note the simultaneous movements in both the social wants, and the social resources and means. A country, let us suppose, is barbarous and sparsely peopled ; we contemplate Persia, or the India of pre-Anglican times. In that low state of civilisation the acknowledged common interests are few, and a land revenue, or the rent of the soil, will suffice to cover the common expenses. Then comes a denser state of population: we contemplate modern European countries; the general expenses of society have grown. But, simultaneously with their growth, grows also the needed nutriment, and wherever the common expenses are, of necessity, heaviest, that is, in great towns and cities, there do these monopolies, of which we have spoken, multiply and wax in remunerativeness. There flourish pauperism and crime, costliest scourges, and there also does the value of land rise highest, and there, too, appear docks, telegraphs, &c., and other natural monopolies, in the most lucrative form. The wants come, and their causes bring also the wherewithal to satisfy them. Sheer pedantry it would be to

limit the expenditure of any State in all circumstances and however trying the emergencies, to
the resources provided by these funds. So long as
there exist pauperism and a permanent criminal
population, so long as there are wars to be waged,
and indemnities to be paid, so long certainly must
we resort to taxes or loans. In times of transition,
too, such as 1859, for instance, was to India, there
may be experienced difficulty in making the
expenditure and revenue of all sorts balance. But
the ideal to which we should strive to attain, and
which may be open to other States less compromised
than England by a long history, seems to be that
which I have described. Though that harmony cannot be practically illustrated here, it may be so
where there is no call to meet emergencies.

De Tocqueville has told us—and it scarcely
needed a De Tocqueville to tell us—that a danger
ahead in democratic times is the danger lest the
power of the government should be employed by
'our masters' in bleeding the rich, and absorbing
the earnings of all those whose means tower above
their neighbours. Communism, or some of its evils,

may invade us under the guise of improved taxation
or a democratic budget.   Graduated income taxes
may be gradients to it.   And truly, when no principle governs the selection of taxes, or the amount
to be taken by means of them, it is hard to convince
the interested that they are pushing taxation to
extremity.   Let those, therefore, who regard the
advent of democracy as inevitable, and who do not
desire to see governments ruling by largesses
extorted from the wealthy by the proletariat,
welcome a revenue system which seems to set
natural limits and barriers to the demands of potent
and rapacious poverty.   Let them recollect that
there is a peril lest future revenue come from the
income tax ; that the majority of the electors are
not subject to it ; that they may encourage resort to
it ; and that, indeed, this danger almost approaches
a certainty, unless we manage to dispense with an
income tax.   Let them embrace with gladness a
system which enlists justice on their side, or rather,
what is different, a consciousness on the part of the
rapacious that justice is against them.   It may
prove well hereafter if the share of the State is

defined almost as sharply as the portion of the capitalist or the labourer.

We see, then, the possibility of government, local and imperial, without taxation. To no transcendental motives does the project appeal. It demands no miraculous draught of administrative talents or public virtues. It is simple and intelligible. It is nothing but giving the body politic the blood which it has secreted. And even those who say that the principle is a barren theory, or that we invoke it too late to apply it, will own that it is in unison with much that goes on around us—with the growing disbelief in *laissez-faire* as sterilely taught of old, the taking over so many branches of industry by the State, the perplexity, strikingly revealed in the report of more than one committee, of how to regulate railways without owning them, the growth of companies of almost State dimensions, and the necessity of investing them with State privileges. Those, too, will admit that revenue reform would become clear, that all scrappy suggestions would be welded into one principle which a child might understand, and that the march of the financier would be certain, if not easy, were there truth and value in this principle, the departure from which has perhaps been not the least of unrecorded errors. I know how far out of the path we and others have strayed, how hard it is to hark back, and how easy it is to speak in three words that which generations of strong minds will not accomplish. We have been putting hills and seas between us and this principle. Not in our time, perhaps never, will they be wholly cast down and utterly dried up. But I still presume to think that it is good to contemplate a splendid possibility, some dim similitude of which may one day be realised, to the unspeakable benefit of society.

I have written the above in deference to the observation of Turgot: 'It is always *the best* with which one ought to be occupied in theory. To neglect this search under the pretext that this best is not practicable in the actual circumstances, is to wish to solve two questions at once; it is to renounce the advantage of placing the questions in that simplicity which can alone render them suscep-

tible of demonstration; it is to plunge without a
clue into an inextricable labyrinth and to wish to
investigate all the routes at once, or rather it is
voluntarily to shut one's eyes to the light by putting
oneself in the impossibility of finding it.' It will be
well, as he advises, to separate the two questions,
' What should be done?' and ' What can be done ? '
Now, if theorists have been prone to exaggerate the
ease with which principles of the above character
could be carried into effect, there has been another
error of an opposite kind. It has been Englishmen's
pride to curtail the interference of the State. We
have been prone to speak of governments as if their
members were not made of flesh and blood, but
were some evil agencies. That State management
must be costly, inefficient, and cumbrous, has been
an axiom with some generations of English poli-
ticians. Now, this assumption, drawn from the
records of Crimea blunders, Admiralty mistakes, and
Ordnance contracts, may have been sound so long
as the choice lay between the State, more or less
lethargic, and private individuals, active and zealous
with the activity and zeal of private interest; it is

not so strong—it is, indeed, of dubious worth—when the choice lies between the State or a municipality and a vast joint-stock company possessed of next to none of the administrative virtues of individuals. Wherein the Erie management excelled the management of the gas-works of Manchester by the corporation, or, to take an instance nearer home and more recent, wherein was the superiority of the management of the Metropolitan Railway over that of the Post Office, is not clear. The excellence of private control is a powerful argument when turned against proposals to make the central government the immediate director of any large and complicated branch of industry—say, to govern all the railways from Downing Street or Whitehall by a department changing with every turn of politics; it loses much of its force when it is directed against proposals to hand over to municipalities the control of such natural or practical monopolies as gas and water works or docks; it is wholly shorn of its strength when it is used against proposals to lease the railways to private individuals or companies, or to grant, as in France, concessions terminable at the expiration of so many years, or against any scheme which would leave the cultivators with almost all their present rights, and which would substitute for private landowners the State. The tenants on the existing Crown domains do not complain of cramping interference; they enjoy at least as much liberty as that accorded by the average English landowner — perhaps, as a rule, they enjoy more; and were the Crown domains ten times as large as they are, there need be no change for the worse.

There are another class of objectors who ex-aggerate the difficulties in the way of realising the principles which have been stated. It has, for ex-ample, been alleged that the nationalisation of the land, to which all that has preceded leads up, would involve an expenditure of 4,500,000,000*l.*, a sum equal to more than seventy years' purchase of the present annual value of the soil. Now, the real obstacles are great enough without clothing them in any such dubious form as the above. Of course, the mere circumstance that the cultivated land in the United Kingdom amounts to

47,000,000 acres [1] puts the acquisition of the whole soil by the State into the far future, even if it do not actually render the task impracticable for ever. So long as it rests with Parliament, chiefly composed of landowners, to determine what shall be the terms on which the purchase shall be completed, only hard terms for the State can be anticipated. Only let us not fall into an error quite as great as that of those who speak of the nationalisation of the soil as a matter of no magnitude, and let us not confound difficulty with sheer, palpable impossibility. The annual value of the land in the United Kingdom assessed to Schedule A was, in 1870, 56,540,000*l.* A perpetual annuity of this amount is equal to a terminable annuity varying in amount with its duration. I apprehend that thinkers such as Mr. Mill would argue that the latter would be a full equivalent of all the landowners' just claims. If he and those of his way of thinking are right, then all which it would be essential to raise would be the difference between the perpetual and the terminable annuity

<hr />

[1] Agricultural Returns for 1872.

for a certain number of years. Those, again, who
allege that such a mode of treatment would be
unfair, inasmuch as it would ignore the reasonable
prospects of a rise in value, would admit that the
value of the fee-simple of an estate at any moment
consists of the value of the life interest together
with that of the reversion, and that if both interests,
or their equivalents, were enjoyed, full compensation
would be given. If then all proprietors received at
the present time the value of the reversions of their
land, and if they were allowed to enjoy their estates
for the period of their lives, they would be compensated. The reversionary value of 1*l.* in perpetuity,
one hundred years hence, at 3 per cent., is 1·7344*l.* ;
and assuming that the annual value of land were
reckoned, not at 56,000,000*l.*, but 60,000,000*l.*,
it would follow that the present payment of
104,064,000*l.* would entitle the State to the ownership a century hence. In other words, an addition of less than one-seventh to the national debt
would suffice to purchase the land as valued under
Schedule A. Of course, if we assume a higher rate
of interest, the outlay would be correspondingly

diminished; assuming $3\frac{1}{2}$ per cent., the sum necessary would be 54,960,000*l*.; assuming 4 per cent.,
it would be 29,700,000*l*. In strict accuracy we
ought, perhaps, to make some subtractions from
the present annual value assigned to the total
landed property. We may have included lands some
of which are of a quasi-public character, and
which need not be bought; and as regards other
portions, so far as they are not vendible—and, in
spite of the new freedom with respect to not
a little land held in mortmain, much is in that
condition—it may be contended that the compensation accorded should be with justice inferior to that accorded to the proprietors of land
which can at any moment be brought into the
market. Nor does the principle stop here. In
proportion to the remoteness of the reversionary
interest does its present value diminish until it
dwindles into an infinitesimally small sum. Mathe-
matically, the reversion of property one hundred and
fifty years hence is worth something; but practically
it is not. Such an interest is not vendible; and the
law would no doubt disregard any arrangement

made with respect to it, for inevitably there would be some violation of the rules against perpetuities. It may, then, be submitted that no existing right meriting compensation would be injured, were this reversion, of no pecuniary value to the present owner, but valuable to the State, which is immortal, appropriated by the latter, and that ample justice would be done by the present payment of a sum which would, one hundred and fifty years hence, yield a perpetual annuity equal to, or slightly in excess of, the present annual value of the soil.

There is another mode which, only give time, would facilitate the same work. It may be shown that if a special tax be imposed upon land, and if it be suffered to subsist, it will, in course of time, cease to be felt as a tax. Land will be bought and sold subject to it; offers will be made, and prices will be settled, with a reference to it; and each purchaser who buys for the purpose of earning the average rate of profit will reduce the purchase money, owing to the existence of the tax. If he does not, it will be because he prefers something to profits. Hence the land tax imposed in 1693

so far as it is not redeemed, has probably ceased to
be felt as a tax. 'It is no more a burden on the
landlord than the share of one landlord is a burden on the other. The landowners are entitled to
no compensation for it, nor have they any claim to
its being allowed for, as part of their taxes.'[1]
Hence, too, it follows that if it was originally fair to
impose a land tax of 4*s.*, it is now fair to add a tax
of the same amount; or, in other words, if the landowner of the reign of Victoria may be justly called
upon to bear as heavy a burden as that borne by
his forefather, the land tax must be raised to 8*s.*,
of which 4*s.* will be a rent-charge or the share of
a joint tenant, and only the remainder will be of the
nature of a tax. *Cæteris paribus*, the landowner's
profits will be as high under the 8*s.* land tax as
were those of his predecessor under the 4*s.* No
doubt it may be said that the landlord's return on
his capital is constantly diminishing.[2] But this
decline is simultaneous with a general lowering of
the rate of profits derivable from all branches

---

[1] J. S. Mill's *Political Economy*, 'People's' Edition, 494.
[2] Thiers, *De la Propriété*, 153.

of industry; and, admitting the facts to be as
alleged, it still would be true that the relative
subtraction from the landowners' incomes owing
to the 4*s.* and the 8*s.* taxes would be the same.
In course of time the same causes which effaced
the first four shillings would remove the weight
of the 8*s.* : whenever land is sold, it will be so with
an eye to the existence of the latter tax. The process will not stop here ; assuming that rents do
not fall, that land is freely sold, that no equivalent
tax is levied upon personalty, and that the increments of taxation are imposed at very distant intervals, in the lapse of time each addition to the land
tax will be shifted from the landowners. Thus it
would seem that there is no taxing them always,
unless the land tax be repeatedly raised, and that, if
such an impost is just at all, the State must in fairness keep whittling at the portion of the landowner
until, at some distant period, it is absorbed by
taxation. It may, indeed, be contended that a
special land tax is always unfair. On the other
hand, it is submitted that, up to the point at
which rent is 'economical,' it may fairly be sub-

jected to special charges. But, whether this statement is right or wrong, it will, we suppose, be
admitted that all taxes on realty which have existed
for many years could not be removed without
bestowing upon the present race of landowners a
large gratuity; and should pauperism be greatly
reduced, and should the imperial and local expenditure be considerably curtailed, this fact may be of
moment with respect to the procuring of funds for
the nationalisation of land.

I presume to think that the acquisition of the soil
by the State seems easier in the light of these simple
truths. Time rather than huge votes of money,
judicious and temperate taxation rather than purchase, may help very much to nationalise the land.

The purchase of reversions, so far as expedient,
and the special taxation of land, seem to be
the chief processes by which the work is to be
accomplished, so far as it is now practicable. To
the latter process there is the objection that it must
operate slowly. Not in much less than sixty years
could it be assumed that the incidence of a tax of
4s. would be removed, owing to buying and selling;

and to absorb a large part of the whole would
require, perhaps, the next century. Purchase of
reversions would be an admirable auxiliary but for
two circumstances, one of which is the uncertainty
of the future value of land. It is too generally
assumed that in England rent has always been
growing in amount. No doubt there may be cited
surprising evidence of the development of the value
of landed property. To judge by Gregory King's
estimate of the annual value of land in England and
Wales in 1688, it has risen six times since that date,
and the rise has gone on of late; for when one looks
into the returns of the property tax, one discerns
an increase not wholly attributable to the additional
breadth under cultivation. Thus, between 1853 and
1870, the annual value of the rent-bearing area of
the United Kingdom increased from 47,559,474*l.* to
56,540,000*l.*—an increase considerable, but not at
all equal to that which houses and mines exhibited
in the same period.[1] At the same time, there have
been, even during the present century, great fluctua-

---

[1] The annual value of houses in the United Kingdom in
1853 was 46,959,338*l.*, and in 1870 82,732,000*l.* The value of
mines in the former year was 2,809,733*l.*, and in the latter
5,840,410*l.*

tions in rents. During the French wars they rose
enormously. After the peace they fell 10 to 33 per
cent. Under the influence of the Corn Laws, they
again rose, to decline, however, for a few years after
the markets of England were thrown open to the
world. From 1852 to the present time they have
steadily risen.[1] But their course hereafter is necessarily uncertain. No one can predict whether or
not land has attained its highest point of value, or,
in other words, whether our population and wealth
will increase, or whether we shall draw more and
more of our food from abroad. So much uncertainty exists, that purchase by the State on the basis
of the present value might prove highly inexpedient,
and it would not be advisable unless there was the
prospect of an advance. The second impediment
to any scheme for acquiring the soil by pur-
chasing the reversions is the fact that it must
operate too slowly, and too clearly demand self-
sacrifice, to be generally interesting or captivating.
Even people who are self-denying for their most

---

[1] For data respecting alterations in the price of land, see
notes to Roscher's *Principles of Political Economy*, vol. ii.
' Rent.' Also Eden's *State of the Poor*, vol. iii.

remote and alien contemporaries have no idea of serving posterity. It is an unborn virtue. But, whatever mode is employed, the interests of those concerned will no doubt be remunerated, now that we have agreed to substitute compensation for revolution. In any event they deserve the treatment of those who have bought that which ought not to have been sold.

We have already stated that most countries have come nearer to realising the above ideal than England. In India the ownership of the soil resides in the State. Not a few other countries have approximated to the same ideal by means of the creation of peasant proprietors, or, in other words, by diffusing the soil as much as possible among the people. In the United Kingdom alone do we see the prevalence of a land system unlike those two: here the State gets little of the rent, and the people at large get little of the land. I venture to think that a closer approximation to both those conditions seen abroad is desirable in England—to the former because it is theoretically just, to the latter because in the interests of order it is expedient that the people should not be severed from the soil.[1] Yet we need not force on the latter state of things ; we may leave events to bring it naturally to pass. Those indeed who would force a system of peasant proprietors upon any country, seem to commit the same mistake as that which ensnares Protectionists, who would foist upon some nation an unsuitable branch of industry. Oftentimes, if successful, they would divert a country from occupations relatively most advantageous; and to do so is to go against the first principles of Free Trade. There are economists who, one cannot doubt, would be disposed to agree with Lord Kames in suggesting the establishment of a tax on all farms requiring three ploughs.[2] There are others who would foster the creation of small farms or peasant properties by lavish public grants. What are they

[1] 'It is better that half the community should, as in Prussia, share even inequitably the theoretical rent, than that only a tenth of the community should, as is probably the case in Great Britain, share inequitably that theoretical rent.' —Mr. Harris-Gastrell's 'Report on Tenure of Land in Prussia.' *Reports Respecting the Tenure of Land Abroad*, part i. p. 444.

[2] *The Gentleman Farmer*, 6th ed. p. 307.

but Protectionists? To me it seems that people must, in the long run, judge rightly as to the propriety of converting their country into a series of peasant properties or small farms. Their judgment, perhaps, will not proceed on the mere fact that the yield per acre of wheat, say in Guernsey, where small farming is carried to perfection, may be fifty-five bushels,[1] while in England, the average return is only about twenty-eight; it will also turn on the question whether the given amount of labour at the disposal of the country might be employed more profitably than in wholly devoting it to agriculture. When pronounced decisively, their judgment will be interfered with only by rash legislators.

[1] Duncan's *History of Guernsey*, p. 294.

CHAPTER IV.

URBAN LAND.

So FAR the principles which ought to govern property in land. Let us proceed to apply them with
an eye to the special circumstances of the various
kinds. There are many reasons why we should
begin with urban land. With respect to it, there is
ample scope and most pressing urgency for the application of the principles which we have stated. In the
ground-rents of cities are to be seen perfect samples
of 'economical rent,' due to monopoly, produced by
no man's labour, assuredly not always by the labour
of the owner of the soil. The rents of houses, so
far as ground-rent is an element therein, are solely
the prices paid for situation, or 'the original and
indestructible properties of the soil.' Thus the
Duke of Bedford and the Marquis of Westminster
exact some hundreds of thousands of pounds

annually from those who enrich their property. They are remunerated because certain land is situated in Middlesex—a circumstance in which one may be pardoned for failing to recognise the beneficent hand of the owner. Of the annual rateable value of London, for instance, computed at 23,000,000*l*., an increasingly large portion is the value of ground-rents. When a square foot of land in Victoria Street lets for one pound sterling, we may judge of the immense revenue flowing from this source into private purses. Those increments scarcely ever proceed solely from the diligent exertions of the proprietors. Were they imbeciles instead of good men of business, they must earn more than thousands of toiling artisans ; were they Solons or Solomons, it would not make much difference. Their position of affluence is independent of virtue or vice, prudence or folly. They exist; that is their service. It was the sole service of most of their ancestors. In the prices paid for sites in cities, we see the most surprising instances of rises in value of that character which Mr. Mill terms the 'unearned increment.' A few examples occur to me. Somewhat marvellous though they

may seem, they cannot be scouted as exceptional. *£160 ... in*
A piece of land in Holborn, purchased in 1552 for *C 5% ... i*
160*l.*, now yields 5,000*l.* a year; a wharf in Castle
Baynard, bought for 2,000*l.* in 1670, lately realised
110,000*l.* ;[1] and an acre of land at South Kensing-
ton, which was sold for 3,200*l.* in 1852, fetched
23,250*l.* in 1860. We are told that the price of an
acre of the most valuable uncovered land in the city
of London after the Great Fire of 1660 'was
30,000*l.*, or about one-third of the value of the land
when built upon. At the present time the highest
rate for unbuilt land may be taken at 1,000,000*l.*
an acre, and such value constitutes fully three-
fourths of the value of the property after it has
buildings upon it.'[2]

Into a very distinct category, meriting special
and primary consideration, the sites of cities are
perhaps placed by reason of another circumstance.
That the local community should acquire them,
is a proposition free from many of the objections
taken to any scheme for the nationalisation of the

[1] Sir Charles Trevelyan on 'The City Parochial Endow-
ments.'

[2] Paper read by Mr. Edmund James Smith, at Institution of
Surveyors, January 29, 1872.

whole land of the kingdom. To propose to buy
in and to govern property, the annual value of
which, as assessed to Schedule A, is 56,000,000*l.*,
may well cause the timid, and even the stouthearted
to recoil. But to endow municipalities with the
power of compulsorily acquiring the dominion of
the soil on which they are established—to permit
them to avail themselves of those vast increments of
purely ' economical rent,' created by their industry
if by anybody's—is a step perhaps unassailable on
the grounds of prudence as well as of justice. It is
not novel or audacious. It has precedents without
number in its favour. And, moreover, were the
rent fund issuing from the soil to be used as a supplement of, or a substitution for, rates, it would be
particularly beneficial to our great towns, which feel
more than country districts, the burden of local
taxes. Their ' increase,' says Mr. Goschen, ' has
approached more nearly to the increase in the rateable value in the four counties, Middlesex, Surrey,
Lancashire, and West Riding, taken together, than
in the remaining counties of England.'[1]   It is the

---

[1] Mr. Goschen's Report on Local Taxation, p. 41.

towns which may with most justice complain of the pressure of taxation; it is the towns which, fortunately, possess the remedy. And for all these reasons, it seems right that we should speak first of the ground-rent of cities.

Perhaps the best way of demonstrating the importance and practical value of the principle is to take a great city, such as London, and to show what advantages would have accrued from the acquisition of the natural monopolies connected therewith. Even if the time has gone by for London to put in operation the principle, other cities may take warning before it is too late. Complaints of the growth of local taxation in London have been loud and frequent, particularly since the establishment of the Metropolitan Board of Works in 1855. Some years ago Sir William Tite declared that the limit of local taxation had been reached. More than one parliamentary committee have borne testimony to the same fact. Impressed with a sense of the onerous weight of the present system of local taxation, and conscious that plans for equalising the rates throughout London were inadequate remedies, Mr. Goschen proposed in 1868 to institute a municipal income-tax, so that the dwellers in the West End parishes might be compelled to furnish their equitable quota ; and, though in 1871 he publicly condemned a local income-tax as necessarily unfair in its incidence, we do not suppose that he has retracted his opinion that the rates fall heavily, and even most heavily, on needy householders.   After all that has been done to introduce a uniform mode of assessing, and notwithstanding the Act which puts on the whole metropolis certain charges on account of the poor, it is still true that the inhabitant of one parish in London may contribute one-tenth of his income to the support of paupers, while the tenant of a town mansion in St. James's Square may not contribute more than one-hundredth.   It is still the case that the weight of the rates impoverishes the poor, and helps to drive them into miserable and degrading dwellings. Sir Sydney Waterlow, chairman of a company started for the purpose of building houses in the East End for the working classes, gave evidence before a parliamentary committee that

inquired into local taxation of the serious impedi-
ments which the height of the rates placed in the
way of the company's labours. And, in order to
raise an income of half-a-dozen millions, it is found
necessary to continue, simultaneously with these
rates, certain taxes of a most questionable character.
Octroi duties, scouted almost everywhere else, are
levied in London. There is a coal duty which
mulcts London and the neighbourhood for twenty
miles around. There is a wine duty; and a portion
of the revenue is derived from brokers' rents, fines,
and fees, and the metage of corn and fruit. So much
for the hardships of those who pay: let us now look
to the indulgence accorded to those who enjoy partial
or total exemption. Of the 75,000 acres covered
by London no small portion is, as every one knows,
let on leases of sixty, eighty, and ninety-nine years.
This form of tenure, to be found on the great
urban estates of the Duke of Bedford, the Duke of
Portland, the Marquis of Westminster, Lord Portman, Lord Carnarvon, Lord Holland, Lord South-
ampton, the Foundling Hospital, &c., has en-
gendered many evil effects, not the least of which

has been to cover so large a space with mean
mansions and stucco palaces, and brick and mortar
sheds, and paltry houses, which age invests with
dirt and dinginess, but hardly with venerableness.
But its chief pernicious effect has been to give to
those proprietors fiscal exemptions which need only
to be universally known in order to be universally
condemned.

What contribution do those proprietors make to
local taxation? It may be asserted that some of
their property contributes absolutely nothing to the
newly-imposed rates and inadequately to the older
rates. The assertion may be proved. At the time
when many of the now running leases of ninety-nine
years were entered into, there could have been no
anticipation of the outlay caused by, and the rates
imposed in consequence of, the Thames Embankment
and the Main Drainage Scheme. These items could
not have formed a factor in old bargains; and such
rates imposed, let us bear in mind, for purposes of
permanent improvement, must have fallen wholly on
those possessing temporary interests—the owners of
houses and the occupiers. It is no doubt true that

at certain periods in the first half of this century, the poor and county-rates were high in Middlesex. Thus, in. 1803, the poor and county-rate, with a portion of the church-rate, amounted to $3s.\ 5\frac{1}{4}d.$, and in 1868 rates of all kinds to $3s.\ 11\frac{3}{4}d.$ But the general tendency has been towards a steady increase of the rates. Nor did those exemptions begin with the imposing of the Metropolitan Consolidated Rate to meet the wants of the Metropolitan Board of Works. One who examines the local or private measures, passed for the most part in the reigns of George III. and George IV., in order to 'pave, cleanse, light, water, and embellish' various squares in London, will find them studded with acts of favouritism to landlords. Looking, for instance, into 7 Geo. IV. c. 58, relating to Grosvenor Place and other lanes and streets adjoining, I find among its 140 clauses, one giving powers to commissioners to compel owners and builders of houses where there ought to be streets to pave, level, or gravel them. But the Act specially exempted Robert, Earl of Grosvenor, from paying for the improvement of his own property. It also empowered him to

put whatever fences or gates he was pleased to
erect on streets which others maintained. A similar
provision appears in many of the Acts passed in
the last century for the purpose of paving or embel-
lishing the various estates on which much of the
west of London is built. Some of the Acts—for
instance, that relating to the Calthorpe estate—
practically absolve the owner of the freehold from
all charges. The ratepayers, in short, were mulcted
in order to improve and 'embellish' the landowners'
estates. It is true that they may occasionally have
done a little paving. Thus, the Duke of Bedford
went to some expense with respect to Oakley Square.
But I find that the Vestry of St. Pancras repaid him.
The facts remain as they are here stated, somewhat
shabby and incredible though they may seem.

Here seems the fit place for adverting to a
circumstance which relates to this part of our theme,
and which will also fall to be noticed in connection
with agricultural land. There is such a thing as the
owner of the ground-rent getting more than 'the
economical rent,' and that, too, permanently. To
suppose otherwise is to suppose what is not always

the fact, that tenants either can, or choose to, bargain at arm's length with their landowners. One
must note a distinction which clearly exists between
letting agricultural land and the sites of cities,
and which it is opportune to mention here.
To the farmer, farming for profit's sake, all
localities may be alike if all are equally cheap;
but to the occupier of a house, oft-times locality
is all-important, and rather than sacrifice a certain
place of abode, he will pay such a rent as virtually
to take on himself the rates. His dearest pleasures
may hang on the situation of his house. And I
think that there is another clear distinction to be
taken on this occasion. The builder and the
owner of the ground will try to make each bargain relative to a house individually remunerative.
To them each sale or leasing is a purely commercial transaction. But the occupier will not
always give so much less rent because the rates
are so much. He will economise, no doubt,
but it may be in regard to railway travelling, or
dress, or dinners, and not necessarily, as is too
frequently assumed, in regard to house rent. Most

men will set a certain limit to their household expenses; but they will not necessarily rigidly define what portion of it will be rent. Further, competition as to the incidence of rates is often competition between those who desire to earn 10 per cent. and those who, having earned 10 per cent., desire to spend it comfortably. And even when it is with some truth alleged that the rates ultimately fall on the landowner, what more in the case of cities does it generally mean than that his 'unearned increment' is slightly diminished, and not that the earned increment is touched? Nor need we stop short at local rates. Of course, in the first instance the occupier pays the income-tax on house property, and the owner is obliged to refund it under a penalty of 50*l.* But that obligation may be nominally kept while it is broken in spirit and effect by raising the rent so as to include the tax, a rent of 105*l.* with the condition of returning 5*l.* being the same to a landlord as a rent of 100*l.* without that condition; and so keen is the competition for houses along the busy thoroughfares or in fashionable quarters that the above contingency is doubtless frequently realised.

To complete the story, let us advert to some
more direct benefits, of which those persons thus
specially exempted are the recipients. It is well
known that there are many streets in London,
particularly in Marylebone, St. Pancras, and Chel-
sea, over which the public possess no complete
rights, and to which they are admitted only on
sufferance. In the urban domains of the Duke of
Bedford, the Marquis of Westminster, and Lord
Portman, there are erected gates which are closed
at odd, early, and inconvenient hours, and which
vindicate the seignorial right to treat some of
the most populous districts of London as if they
were private gardens. Curious and absurd are
some of the prohibitions contained in the Bedford
ukases. For instance, no hearse or funeral proces-
sion may pass through Gordon Square—a fact
which the friends of a deceased tenant of the Bedford estate discovered on the day of the funeral
to their chagrin. At not a few turnings stand
ducal beadles ready to turn back plebeian vehicles,
and to bar the way against short-cuts at late or
early hours. A recent Parliamentary return

showed the number of these gates to be still very great, particularly on the Bedford estate. They are, as a rule, due to private Acts of Parliament which I have already referred to, passed in the reigns of George III. and George IV., for the purpose of paving, cleansing, and lighting streets laid out on private estates. It was by the same legislation that it came to pass that St. Pancras alone had sixteen paving boards, eleven of which, filled with nominees of the freeholder, were self-elected. The Metropolitan Local Management Act, which committed the office of paving to the vestries, swept these boards away, and the sole reminiscence of the extinct bodies consists of the bond debts which they incurred, and which still remain to burden certain districts. In the above Act, the influence of the landlords was powerful enough to insert a clause reserving their right to maintain gates. What is the net result of the history? This: by private Acts the proprietors originally got their estates paved by the occupiers: the mainten-ance and repair of the streets from which the public are partially excluded, is and was the work of the public, each district receiving the benefit of the general rate levied over the whole of the metropolis; and, to complete the job, the value of the sites along the streets is artificially enhanced by the maintenance of gates, which, giving privacy, and creating a *rus in urbe*, enable the freeholder to exact a higher rent. In the face of all this, which is more marvellous, the patience of those who tolerate it, or the effrontery of those who flaunt their tyrannical placards before passers-by?[1]

Much of the increase in the rates of London is attributable to the Main Drainage Scheme and the Thames Embankment. Of the latter it cannot be said that even temporarily it benefited the dwellers in the East-end, certainly not in any other sense than that in which it was for the advantage of the inhabitants of Reading or Exeter: all London occupiers,

---

[1] Of course, at the expiration of the leases, the houses fall to the owner of the soil; and I may here mention that this power has been too frequently grossly abused. There is recorded the case of a noble lord—some former Lord Somers, I believe —who first of all threatened to claim a forfeiture a few years before the end of the leases, unless certain important repairs were effected, and who, at the close of the lease, coolly and rapaciously appropriated houses and repairs.

however, furnished their quota, while many of the owners, whose property will be permanently and enormously enhanced in value, contributed nothing. This fact, which a Parliamentary Committee some years ago mildly characterised as ' contrary to sound policy,' is sad enough, but worse has yet to be told. The Marquis of Salisbury and the other proprietors of the land along the line of the Embankment received from the Metropolitan Board of Works ample compensation for the wharves and buildings which were destroyed or appropriated in the course of the work. But subsequent events have brought them compensation of an indirect but very substantial character. No sooner was the Embankment formed than the remainder of their property, opened up for building purposes, was vastly increased in value.

Instead of spending time in depreciating a system of privileges with which there is mixed up so much injustice, though no one concerned, perhaps, is acting with conscious unfairness, let us turn to the remedies. The Parliamentary Committee that admitted these flagrant facts to be ' contrary to sound policy,' proposed that the rates should be, as in Scotland, paid, half by the owner and half by the occupier. Such a scheme would alleviate many of the evils complained of. But it would be far from doing all that is needful. It would not undo the past. Private individuals would still absorb ground, or purely economical, rent. The poor would still be driven into miserable dwellings by the pressure of taxation; still would the lords of the soil escape their fair burthen; and still to him that hath would be given in most unscriptural abundance. More seems necessary; and were we living in 1800, and not in 1873, the right course would have been plain and rather easy. Had the wants of the future, and the growth of London, been foreseen, and had it not then, as now, been 'a province covered with houses,' with no government extending over the whole area, it might have been for the interest of the community to take over at valuation large tracts which have since been built upon. We have stirred late, and we cannot now move with ease. But something may yet be done in the right direction; and when

London possesses a local government superior to that formed by the Local Management Acts, and similar to that which Mr. Mill has proposed, we may take the first great step. Here, if anywhere, there is a sphere and an occasion for the application of Mr. Mill's theory of the unearned increment. Here, in the most flagrant form, is that divorce between industry and earnings which breeds communism; and those who hesitate to urge the acquisition of the entire soil by the State, may fearlessly put in operation their principles with respect to London and other great cities. For we are not quite too late. Justice may be done, and even generosity accorded, to all concerned, and yet we may be drawing near, at no mean speed, to that ideal time in which the soil shall belong to the community. To those whose land is let on leases which have twenty years or more to run, we might give a promise that they should not be touched during that period, and at the close of it we might come to them and say, ' The present value shall be yours, any additional value shall belong to the community. You have had your time; it is the ratepayers' turn to have theirs.' To those, on the other hand, whose leases had less than twenty years to run, and whose calculations and reasonable prospects might be obscured by the earlier application of the principle, we might grant a respite. To all, however, sooner or later, we should mete out the same justice : future increments should be the community's. This would be the first application of the process of absorption. But in order to ensure that no hardship be inflicted, let a period of reprieve be given.

In the second place, it might be expedient to invest cities with the power of acquiring the land on which they are situated, without being obliged to resort to Parliament. And, no doubt, it would sometimes appear expedient, as already suggested, to purchase the reversion rather than the fee simple. It need not be said that the acquiring of a municipal revenue from rent is no novelty. The city of London, in this respect like Liverpool, the borough fund of which is large, obtains much of its receipts from that source. Madox, in his '*Firma Burgi*,' gives many instances of cities that dispensed more or less with rates, by acquiring from the Crown rights over the soil.[1]

Even before cities, as such, possess the right to acquire their sites by compulsory purchase, they may do much to become the proprietors thereof by certain auxiliary means. The formation of a great public work, such as the Victoria Embankment, necessarily enhances the value of the adjacent property, and it seems strange that Parliamentary powers should not be regularly taken to obtain the adjacent plots opened up by public works at prices to be governed by the value *before* the improvements. It is stated by Mr. Frederic Hill that by the adoption of this expedient the municipality of Hamburg managed to rebuild the city destroyed by fire, on a plan far superior to the former, at a cost of ' about a thousand pounds.'[2] It was applied to Victoria Street with great advantage. If only

---

[1] 'Towns, like communes or parishes, are corporative associations in Germany, that hold property, frequently in land and houses, often in mills and other possessions.' ' This wise system of co-operative association,' 'is the oldest of which we have any record.'—Banfield on *The Manufactures of the Rhine*, p. 132.

[2] *The Land Question*, by Frederic Hill.

the ratepayers of London be alert, there is still another device open to them, and useful in co-operating with the expedients already named. On certain of the great estates in London, the occupiers pay, in addition to the general rate, devoted to paving, lighting, &c., an exceptional impost, for the purpose of meeting the interest and clearing off the principal of the bonds issued by the defunct Paving Commissioners. On some estates the debt is wiped out; on others it is still large. At intervals the bonds are paid off, and the special rate wholly or partially drops. Of course, the frequent, though not the universal, result is that rent rises, and that at the end of the lease the freeholder is empowered to exact a larger ground rent. As these debts are of old standing, the mere removal of them would be tantamount to vast gifts to the freeholders. Now, if that be true, perhaps it would be right to main-tain those special rates as so many great deductions from rent, and credit their proceeds to the local treasuries. I observe that on the Duke of Bedford's estate, within the jurisdiction of St. Pancras Vestry, there is a debt of 26,374*l.*, and that there is a rate of

3*d*. in the pound, designed to act as a sinking fund.[1]
If rents on the Bedford estate have been levied
with an eye to the existence of this tax, the result
may be, when the bonds are liquidated, and this
rate lapses, an increase in the total rental of the
Bedford estate to the amount of that sum ; and I
submit that the parish might reasonably be permitted by Parliament to maintain these charges,
even after the purposes for which they were originally imposed have been satisfied.   At all events,
let us consider whether we are prepared to make a
fresh gift to that ' leviathan among all the creatures
of the Crown,' the House of Bedford.   This matter
is   too   important   to   be   discussed   on   personal
grounds, but it is fair to ask what has been effected
by recent owners to justify another subsidy.   ' Who
ever saw the Duke of Bedford ? ' used to be asked
by the tenants of a former Duke, and the question is
still pertinent.

So far the land on which our great cities are
built.   But land is not the only monopoly available

---

[1] Abstract of cash received and expended by the Vestry of
St. Pancras, Middlesex.

for their use. And I may be permitted to refer here, for the sake of completeness, to a few others. The docks of London are owned by private companies. Yet, at their outset, the East India and the West India Docks received at the hands of Parliament monopolies of the trade with the East and West Indies. These companies have at various times amalgamated after severe struggles, which have not always left them in a very flourishing condition. The example of the Liverpool Dock Trust shows the possibility of a public body managing such concerns; and there can be little doubt that if the London docks had been built by the municipality, if there had been no wasteful war of competition, and if they had never been saddled with the expense of some eighty-six directors, they would have yielded a revenue of fully a million. Certainly that sum might have been derived from them and the private wharves. At various times it has been proposed that the Metropolitan Board of Works, or some other representative of the ratepayers, should acquire the gas-works, another species of monopoly. I may speak of them as such, because, though from 1842 down to 1860 the Legislature permitted competition—four companies, for instance, competing in Regent Street—the principle of 'districting' the companies has been faithfully observed since the latter year; and within its own area, each of the thirteen gas companies enjoys an undisturbed monopoly, and earns a large dividend with regularity. The idea of the municipality supplying gas—an idea long ago and most successfully carried out in Manchester—was contemplated · when Lord Llanover was First Commissioner of Works; in 1867 a Select Committee reported in favour of the principle of the project; and the day of its realisation does not seem, in view of the present dissatisfaction with the gas companies of London, so very distant. Considerations even more vital and pressing than any which finance can prompt, urge the adoption of the same policy with respect to the water supply. In this department, says a recent Royal Commission, 'the supercession of the municipalities by joint-stock companies is a comparatively modern innovation.' On many grounds, sanitary ones in particular, that Commission urged the restoration

of the 'ancient practice ; ' and we may add that the
Public Health Act of 1848, and the Local Government Act of 1858, give facilities to public bodies to
acquire water-works. Now that it is known how
much the propagation of disease depends on the
character of the water supply, we may be sure that,
urged by the strongest of motives, communities will.
take into their own custody these gates of life and
death ; and many who will never think of the
principle here submitted, will unwittingly, but
zealously, co-operate in bringing about its consum-
mation.

CHAPTER V.

AGRICULTURAL LAND.[1]

WHY do the landlords of this country enjoy its soil, to the exclusion of the rest of the community? Why can a stranger to the land, a resident, it may be, in London or Paris, legally and morally, exact one pound or two pounds an acre from all who would cultivate a certain farm in Yorkshire or Ulster? Nine out of ten persons to whom these elementary questions are addressed will answer that the landlord or his representatives, in point both of law and equity—some vendor fairly paid or some ancestor of the present owner making a valid devise—brought the land to its present state of cultivation. He drained the land, once a swamp or morass; he fenced the open wold or moor, once

[1] The substance of a part of the following chapter appeared in the *Fortnightly Review* for May 1872.

free to all comers to roam over; often it was he who erected the barns, stables, and farm-steading in general, and out of the rent of one or two pounds, well scrutinised, there is, perhaps, not one farthing which is other than the interest on the capital or labour of the landlord, his ancestor, or a vendor of the estate. This is the popular philosophy of the rights of landowners; it is also, by the way, substantially the reasoning of Locke and not a few philosophers.[1]

Let us examine it in the light of the history of English agriculture. I think that those who repeat the above theory, and who regard the existing rights of the landowner as all based on the same simple and sacred principle as that which consecrates the right to a chattel, the product of a man's own skill or labour, cannot be aware of the presence in the

[1] It is also the philosophy popular with the landowners. 'In England, the landlord, as a rule, did all permanent improvements; the exception was when they were done by the tenant.' Sir Massy Lopes, in the Devon and Cornwall Chamber of Agriculture. *Mark Lane Express*, January 30, 1871. 'In Scotland all permanent improvements are done by the landlords.' Duke of Argyll, House of Lords, June 14, 1870.

statutes, the Common Law, and in English history,
of a mass of evidence at variance with this popular
compendium of the origin and justification of the
landlord's prerogative. It is curious indeed that
this theory should still be repeated, when there lie
spread out to the view of all numerous facts irrecon-
cilable with it. Apart altogether from remote
considerations touching the manner in which the
landowners became possessed of their functions,
dismissing as too alien from modern times the
question of the propriety of any original grant and
appropriation, it can be shown that neither they nor
their representatives in the past have been the .
exclusive improvers and fertilisers of the soil. It is
dubious, in truth, whether they have been the chief
improvers. Others have laboured, and often they
have entered into the fruits of that labour. Many
of the improvements which do not bring immediate
returns,—his alleged peculiar fitness for executing
which is the popular apology for the breadth and
extent of the rights of the landlord,—perhaps would
not have been now accomplished, and might have
been indefinitely delayed, but for the State's assistance,

or, in other words, but for subsidies to the landowners coming from the taxpayers. As to less
arduous works, exacting a small outlay of capital,
and bringing compensation quickly, many of these
have been executed by leaseholders, or even tenants-
at-will. Such is still often the case. Often when
the landowner seems to be the improver, and to
bear the costs, appearances are deceptive, for the
tenant's rent is augmented, and it is he who in
reality bears the burden.

To prove and illustrate these assertions, let me,
in the first place, recall some evidence that the
drainage of the country, both arterial and surface,
is due in a very great degree, directly or indirectly, to the State. From well-nigh the earliest
times of which we have record, the draining or
managing of the sewers (sea-weirs) of the country
has been regarded as a portion of the business of
the Government. One not familiar with the eastern
counties of England can scarcely realise the importance of this agency in some young countries. With
a humid climate, and a low water-shed, and dull
rivers trailing their slow, ill-defined way to the

sea, and steeping the meadows so as to make them resemble the Dutch polders, there is no possibility of effective tillage unless arduous preliminary works are effected, and unless it is somebody's business to maintain these works when once executed. We are apt, too, to be unmindful of the extent to which embankments against the sea were needed, especially along the east coast. Some parts of these counties, such as the Great Level of the Fens, have been pulled ashore. It has been hard work to keep others from going out to sea. Romney Marsh has really been as much made as the Great Eastern, or the London, Chatham, and Dover Railway. 'It was not only the custom,' says Mr. Woolrych, in his work on sewers, 'but their (the Government's) duty also, to save and defend the realm against the sea, as well as against enemies, so that it should be neither drowned nor wasted.' For the supervision of this department of drainage, there was no need of special enactments. It was part of the Common Law that the Crown should undertake its supervision, and when the embankments gave way, the sheriff could impress the labour of the county. In fact, there naturally grew up in Romney Marsh a code of customs subsequently made binding elsewhere. For the formation of inland sewers, on the other hand, it was necessary to resort to Parliament. 'Sewers for the melioration of land,' observes Lord Hale on this head, 'were by act of parliament.' The first important enactment relative to inland drainage is the 6 Henry VI. c. 5. It empowered the Lord Chancellor to grant Commissions of Sewers, with authority to impose rates. The bulk of the provisions of this act were incorporated in the 23 Henry VIII. c. 5, the act which, somewhat amended, is the basis of the authority of the existing Sewer Commissioners. The preamble of this statute promises enormous ameliorations. The draughtsman rises into eloquence, and almost poetry, while he descants on the losses and damages inflicted by the ' outrageous surges ' and the ' outrageous springs.' Robert Callis, a learned lawyer, who prelected on this statute at Gray's Inn, loses his head in contemplating the benefits wrapped up in the folds of this statute. It was, indeed, the fashion for ancient writers of legal text-books, such as Coke or Littleton,

to put a few sprigs of rhetoric and philosophy in
their works, just as it is for many a modern professor
to put a flower on his desk ; but Callis, in defiance
of the nature of his subject, and far in excess
of the fashion of his time, swathes himself in
rhetorical foliage. Nevertheless, we are assured that
the act produced by no means great results.   Its
scope was much restricted by the action of the courts
of law, which chose to construe it as having reference
only to improvements of the channels of navigable
rivers, and which declined to sanction charges imposed
with a view to carry out drainage of a novel character.   If this paper were designed to be a history of
drainage in England, it would be necessary to speak
of the services rendered by James I. and Charles I.,
the former of whom brought over and employed
Cornelius Vermuyden, a skilful Dutch engineer.   It
would also be essential to dwell upon the 13 Elizabeth, c. 9.   In this brief narrative I may, however,
pass by these details ; and of the numerous acts
continuing or amending the above named, I need
mention only one, the 3 & 4 William IV. c. 22,
which empowered the Commissioners, with the con-

sent of the owners and occupiers of three-fourths of the land affected, to raise rates for certain agricultural and other purposes. By whom were the rates, raised under the above statutes, paid? That is the point most material to this inquiry. Under the statute of Henry VIII. the rates were contributed by tenants as well as by the owners. The expressions employed in the act are very general : ' He which hath tenements, profits, rents, common of pasture, profits of fishery, or other commodities ; or such as have safety, profit, defence, or other commodity.' Indeed, the owners were rated only exceptionally. It may be contended that the ultimate incidence of the taxes was on the owners, an abatement in rent ensuing whenever the occupier was assessed. But this tendency, if operative at all, was neutralised by at least two circumstances: the rates were uncertain, and they could not be foreseen when the landlord and tenant bargained, if bargain they did ; and the Commissioners were appointed from among the landowners.

While thus helping to augment the value of land, the State had up to this period been content to empower landowners to rate recalcitrant members of their own class or their tenants. In tracing briefly the history of subsequent legislation, it is unnecessary to do more than refer to the fact that there were passed various acts for the formation of companies, furnished with power to issue debentures, in order to drain such tracts as Cambridge Fens. Private drainage companies still exist. In virtue of special acts owners with limited interests are permitted to charge their estates with loans from these companies for the purpose of improvements, and such charges take priority. In the beginning of this reign the Legislature began two kinds of novel operations. The wonderful results accomplished by Mr. Smith of Deanstoun's method of draining were then exciting much attention. Sir Robert Peel preached the advantages of draining, and practised his teaching. On his own estate he drained two thousand nine hundred acres, and to all his tenants he offered to drain their farms at his own expense on condition that they paid four per cent. on the outlay. The distress of Ireland being then sore and grievous, the necessity of exceptional intervention on

the part of the Legislature being then generally
admitted, philanthropy came to swell the existing
eagerness to drain. It was argued that the bogs
of Ireland were the great source of her poverty.
A select committee of the House of Lords in 1830
recommended drainage at the public expense as
highly expedient. One way in which this eagerness
showed itself was, as we have seen, in interference with
entails. By the 3 & 4 Vic. c. 55, and the 8 & 9 Vic.
c. 56, as well as by the acts applying to Scotland,
landlords who were only tenants for life were permitted to charge their estates with money to be expended in drainage. As the State did not furnish
the money, there was no clear objection to be taken
to the principle of this proposal. The chief flaws in
these acts were of a very different character; they did
not enable the tenant for life to charge the land for
a sufficiently long period. A term of eighteen years
for the repayment of all instalments was too short.
But in principle these acts were perhaps expedient.
The Legislature had allowed entails to be created.
Too many of the landlords, being tenants for life,
found themselves debarred from either charging

their land or selling any portion in order to raise
money to be expended on improvements, and as
selling was naturally unpalatable to a parliament
of landowners, the only alternative was permission to charge one's land.   By the 9 & 10 Vic.
c. 101, however, a new era was opened for the
English landowner.   'Whereas,' says the preamble
of this act, the first of a series of eleemosynary
statutes, known as the Public Money Drainage Acts,
which absolved the English landlords from a not
unimportant portion of their duties, ' it is desirable
that works of drainage should be encouraged, in
order to promote the increased productiveness of the
land and the healthiness of the districts where it is
required, and to supply the demand for agricultural
labour, especially at that season of the year when
other sources are expended, &c.'   This preamble, so
redolent of an old-world Political Economy, was the
strange language used by a parliament of which
Cobden and Joseph Hume were members.   Clearly
the landlords were not to surrender the Corn Laws
without some solid equivalent.   The fear that under
a *régime* of free trade the farmers of England would

be unable to endure foreign competition—a fear which induced Peel generously to offer to his tenants a reduction of rent in some cases—weighed with Parliament, and quieted its scruples against granting this measure of relief to the landowners, and the result was that 2,000,000*l.* were allotted to the landowners of Great Britain and 1,000,000*l.* to those of Ireland. It was decided that the rate of interest under this act should not exceed six and a half per cent.; this also constituted a sinking fund, which would wipe out the debt to the State in twenty-two years. Then came the acts of 1856 and 1861, the latter of which empowered the Treasury to advance sums in aid of improvements certified to be permanent. Let me mention, in conclusion, as belonging to the category of private drainage measures, the act of 1864, which considerably augmented the number of objects for which a land-owner could charge his estates. Such, in brief, is the history of legislation with respect to drainage in England.

As to the terms on which advances were made, I need scarcely say they were below the market rate.

That they were ever accepted, trammelled as they were by numerous conditions respecting the time within which the work was to be completed, and as to the depth of drains, a depth not universally approved — the four-feet drains being often thought unsuitable in certain situations—proves so much of the assertion. But in further corroboration of the statement that the landlords really got gratuities, let me recall the fact that the rate for advances in England under the 9 and 10 Vic. c. 101, was confessedly chosen with an eye to the necessities and poverty of Irish landlords, and that advances were made on the same terms in England and Scotland, where the same degree of distress did not exist. As Lord John Russell observed, in the course of his explanation of the proposal, the rate of advances from the Treasury had, until the passing of the act, been five per cent.; it was reduced to about three and a half per cent. And what, of course, added to the ease of the terms was the facility with which remissions were granted. Of the 10,732,380*l*. 1*s*. 5*d*. actually advanced for purposes more or less connected with Irish agriculture, 5,719,757*l*. 6*s*. were remitted:

and though the major part of the sum was expended on the county relief works, there can be no doubt that these works to some extent absolved the owners of the soil from burdens elsewhere ultimately borne by them.

Under various acts the Enclosure Commissioners in England, and the Commissioners of Public Works in Ireland, were permitted to dole out bounties; and since the unavailing protests of Mr. Roebuck and Mr. Joseph Hume there has been lifted up against them scarcely a voice. It is a rarity to hear a statesman of eminence like Lord Derby expressing a doubt whether they have been beneficial. Nobles and wealthy men took advantage of those State-given facilities, to be paralleled only in Prussia, another country in which the landowners have had a large share in the making of laws. In the reports of the Irish Public Work Commissions, you find the Marquis of Waterford among the borrowers and subsidized agriculturists. I shall use no harsh terms; I shall not call these grants measures of outdoor relief to the landowners; but it may be permitted to one to say without

offence that it is curious to observe that, in times
when the doctrines of free trade have become
household truths, and in a country where the
aspirations of Socialism are most emphatically
disowned, the one occupation to which the State
has freely and almost without cavil or challenge
granted subventions, for which the State has per-
formed that which Socialists have in vain demanded
for other trades, and that the occupation thus
singled out for distinction is one which less than all
others requires State aid. Bounties to new manufactures are ever questionable; but bounties to the
oldest of trades, and the only indigenous one!
Again and again artizans or their friends have
requested loans to be made to them on easy terms
in order to aid them in founding co-operative
institutions. Almost uniformly have their requests
been rejected and derided. Political Economy was
against them, as in its time, and in the mouths of
some expositors, it has been against most things:
their requests were the rank, noisome weeds of
Socialism. In France the friends of co-operation
did indeed obtain a meagre grant in 1848, and no

reproaches have been spared the National Assembly for voting 120,000*l.* to needy artizans who sought to redeem themselves from the uncertainties of the condition of wage-receivers—reproaches not always founded on the imperfect security which they could furnish to the lenders, or on the alleged superfluous character of the occupations, but on some supposed mysterious breach of the principle of justice. I, for one, fail to perceive the existence of any distinction in point of principle, between building barns for a nobleman and warehouses for a group of artizans, or, at all events, it is not clear that those who cut in with a stingy *distinguo* can make out that the difference redounds. to the credit of the landlords possessed of property always more or less convertible, and therefore with some capital always at their disposal. Granted that the community is peculiarly interested in the cultivation of the soil; are the landlords, sitting rent-free for ever, incapable of performing work which tenants will often execute for themselves if allowed a lease of nineteen or twenty-one years wherein to reimburse themselves? and could not a loan, if loan were necessary, go directly into the pockets of the farmer? In order to disarm the above facts it will, no doubt, be contended that, after all, such contributions were small in amount in comparison with what was actually paid out of the private pockets of the landowners. But a detailed examination of both England and Scotland will, it is submitted, fail to justify the contention ; and so far as Ireland is concerned that assertion will probably not be made by those conversant with the country or the authoritative reports of Lord Devon's Commission or Dr. Hancock. So far as drainage has been executed by private funds, the tenants, not the owners, have been the chief contributors. Much land has been drained by farmers unaided. Often they are grateful if, at the termination of leases of nineteen years, if lease of that length there be, a revaluation and a rise of rent do not occur. A very common arrangement is that in virtue of which the owner gives the tiles or pipes, and the tenant furnishes the necessary labour. Even when the landlord bore the whole expenses he obtained two advantages—first, money at a low rate ; secondly, if a tenant for life, liberty to charge what was not his own. But usually he obtained a third advantage—he threw the incidence of the loan, either wholly or partially, on his tenant. Sometimes he made a profit by certain sharp practices. Mr. Caird, in his work on English agriculture, speaks of Yorkshire landlords who borrowed at six and a half per cent. from the Government, and lent at seven and a half per cent. to their farmers. Take the county of Elgin and the adjacent counties as illustration. While the Government loan lasted, the following, as I am kindly informed by one well qualified to speak, was the rule :—' Some proprietors charged their tenants six per cent., but the great majority charged only five. The tenants paid this to the end of their lease, and then their farms were revalued for the coming lease.' Another informant, speaking of the same district and same subject, says the custom was ' to charge the tenant a yearly percentage of about one or one and a half per cent. in excess of the Government rate.' In fact, in a great many instances in which apparently the landlord, or the landlord aided by the State, is the improver, the burden of the work is really borne by the tenant. The latter, too, frequently openly performs the whole work. The authority whom I first quoted adds, ' the tenants have drained a great deal themselves without any help from the proprietors or any one else—perhaps a third, if not a half, of all that has been done. They have expended an equally large portion, too, on buildings, trenching, &c.' One of the greatest works of drainage ever accomplished in the north of Scotland has been accomplished solely by a tenant farmer. The loch of Auchlossan, situated about thirty-five miles west of Aberdeen, was, I recollect, ten years ago a sheet of water two to five feet deep and covering one hundred and eighty acres. There was a margin of sixty acres composed of bog and swamp. It was not the three proprietors of this worthless tract who drained it. A tenant farmer, Mr. James Barclay,[1] undertook and accomplished the task. The feeders of the loch were cut off, a tunnel of three quarters of a mile was excavated to carry off the water, open ditches were dug across

---

[1] Now M.P. for Forfarshire.

the surface of the loch, furrow drains were then made, and for the first two years the whole surface was turned over with the spade at a cost of twenty shillings to sixty shillings an acre. In consideration of this enormous outlay it was stipulated that the tenant should hold this useless piece of land rent-free for twenty years, and should pay one hundred pounds for each of five subsequent years. The proprietors have, however, I understand, extended the period to twenty-seven years. A somewhat similar arrangement exists, I believe, on some of the estates of the Marquis of Huntly. A lease of thirty years is given to the tenant; during the first part of the lease he may pay two shillings and sixpence, then five shillings, and finally a much larger sum.[1]

A second modification of the popular theory of landowning is necessary. This second deduction is as important as the first. It has always been a

---

[1] The Duke of Richmond stated in the House of Lords (June 14, 1870), that a twenty-one years' lease gave sufficient time to obtain compensation for all improvements. His tenants, I can testify, will tell a different tale.

part of the Common Law that improvements, whether in the shape of tillage or manures, buildings or fences erected by the tenant, and, in fact, fixtures generally, become the property of the owner of the soil, in virtue of the maxim, *Quidquid plantatur solo cedit solo.* Though somewhat altered from its old harshness to the advantage of the tenant, that rule, the fit appendage of a land system dependent on slaves or villeins, still subsists. Of course, a custom to the contrary will overrule the doctrine ; and, fortunately, in several of the counties of England, such as Sussex, Surrey, Lincoln, and parts of Kent and Nottinghamshire, there do exist tolerably well-defined customs, in virtue of which the tenant obtains compensation for the unexhausted improvement which he has effected. The doctrine of the Common Law relative to emblements, or growing crops, is another rude and inadequate attempt to mitigate the rigour and injustice of the principle. As a matter of fact, too, landlords dare not use all the power with which the law invests them; public opinion would be shocked were they to do all that which they may do, for here most conspicuously the law, which ought to be abreast if not ahead of the popular morality, lags behind. But not only are these controlling customs far from general in England, and almost unknown in Scotland—their codification, or even the cataloguing of them, would be of great service to landlords and outgoing or ingoing tenants—but it is rare that they meet all causes of complaint.

Though the act of 1851, relative to agricultural fixtures, has to some extent alleviated certain grievances, it is still the case that the tenant who may 'erect any farm building, either detached or otherwise, engine or machinery, either for agricultural purposes or trade and agriculture, without having first obtained the consent of the landlord in writing, does so at the peril of confiscation.' Even if consent is granted, the landlord has a prior right to purchase the machinery and engine at a valuation. Nor are there wanting some signal instances of wrong coming to pass, in consequence of this doctrine. In proof I may refer to the treatment of Dr. O'Fay, parish priest of Craughwell, in the county of Galway, who expended 400*l.* in the erection of buildings, on the

strength of a promise given by the father of his
landlord that a lease should be granted. He was
evicted. His claims were disregarded. He appealed
to no purpose ; the Irish Lord Chancellor, the Lord
Justice of Appeal, and the Master of the Rolls, con-
demning severely the injustice of the law which they
were forced to administer. It is not long since the
Duke of Buccleuch endeavoured in a Scotch court
to appropriate a wire fence erected by a tenant. It
is, however, unnecessary at this point to discuss the
justice or policy of the law relative to fixtures and improvements. It is enough for my present purpose to
draw attention to the operation of this agency in
English agriculture, and to maintain that in the case
of tenants, often compelled to find their sustenance in
farming, without chaffering about terms, and often
unprovided with the security of leases, or, at all
events, leases fortified by tenant-right,[1] the operation

<hr />

[1] For some valuable information respecting leases, see Mr.
Clement Cadle's essay on the Farming Customs and Covenants
of England in the *Journal of the Royal Agricultural Society*,
vol. iii. ; and Mr. Wingrove Cook on *Agricultural Tenancies*.
I may also refer to Mr. McNeil Caird's admirable pamphlet on
The Land Tenancy Laws.

of this rule must have been, and always must be, to transfer to the owner of the soil value which was in reality the product of the labour and capital of the tenant. There being too often no freedom of contract between the two parties, in any other sense than there is between the man who must buy and the man who need not sell, there has not always been the ability to stipulate for compensation for improvements. With more people seeking farms than farmers, and power to evict existing without corresponding ability to stand out for better terms, with needy tenants—whom the law of distress in England, and that of hypothec in Scotland, make it safe to accept—there has been a steady flow of the outlay of tenants into the purses of the landowners. The many generous members of this class, who would scorn to take advantage of the injustice of the law, must not hide from us the few who, give them a chance, would exact the last farthing on the plea that ' business is business.' About the extent of this transference, it is difficult to speak precisely. Surmise must here eke out information. Mr. Caird speaks of the value of the unexhausted improvements

as being, in some English counties, 3*l.* to 5*l.* an acre.
The experience of Ireland throws some dim light on
the problem.[1]   There an outgoing tenant has been
known to sell his right in thirty acres indifferently
tilled for 300*l.*   The total value of the tenant-right
in Ulster has been computed at many millions ; and,
after making allowance for the fact that of the price
paid a part was given for good-will, and taking into
account the well-known truth, mentioned by the
Devon Commission, that in Ireland the tenant has
long been accustomed to execute work elsewhere executed by the landlord, we shall nevertheless arrive at
the conclusion that the sum at stake must be considerable.   Let us here briefly consider two questions.
First : What are the varieties of agricultural capital
which it takes the longest time to replace?   Apart
from drains and buildings, both of which are often
the work of the tenant, probably the articles which
will be longest in recouping themselves will be
threshing machines, or other expensive agricultural

---

[1] The summary of the evidence taken before the Devon
Commission states that ‘ the price of a tenant-right frequently
amounts to 10*l.*, 12*l.*, 20*l.*, or 25*l.* per acre.’

instruments. The second question is this : Of the
entire capital sunk in a well-tilled farm, at any
moment, what constitutes the greater part? Manures, stock, implements, &c.—in other words, all
which it is customary for the tenant to contribute.
So much is the tenant expected to do that Lord
Derby has stated, perhaps a little incautiously, and
with a candour which all his friends will not laud,
that the chief duty of the landlord is, not to hinder
the investment of capital in the land by his tenant.
Without criticising this doctrine that it is the chief
duty of the landowner to keep his hands off his
tenants, I may here cite, with relevancy and propriety, an observation of Mr. J. J. Mechi, of Tiptree
Farm. 'On my farm,'—and, of course, his is
somewhat exceptional experience—'which requires
plenty of manure and deep cultivation, I cannot
prosper with less than 16l. per acre.' I understand
that in Aberdeenshire the tenant should have 6l. to
8l. per acre, in order to cultivate his farm with
success. If the facts be so, and if our answers to
the above questions be correct, this, then, is the
paradox which we find : for the exercise of his

vocation the tenant must have some, nay much, capital, while the landlord need have none, and the law is so framed that the more the former invests the better is the position of the latter.

The numerous modifications which it is imperative to make in the popular theory of property in land have brought one face to face with the conclusion that much of the rent of agricultural land proceeds from the exertions of others than the landowners. But I desire particularly to press home another truth, and that is, that agricultural rent tends more and more to approximate to the condition of ground-rent, or, in other words, to become rent strictly so called. In many of the older counties, and on the estates of landowners who do not improve, it has reached that state. When drainage ceases to be necessary; when the chief advances essential to be made are such as will be returned within a lease of seven to twenty-one years; when the tenant-farmers are a class possessed of capital, and doing the work formerly and properly discharged by the landowners; or when the State or a tenant executes permanent and tardily remunerating improvements, rent, ceasing to be the interest on the capital of the owner, becomes that *produit net* which, we have seen, in equity belongs to the community. When Lord Derby tells his class that its prime duty is to grant leases and let the farmers alone, and when we are assured by the friends of the landowners that the sole reforms necessary are tenant-right and leases, there unwittingly escapes an acknowledgment that agricultural rent is becoming more and more the price charged for a natural monopoly and not a service. It may be true that the benefit of original advances remains; but if the benefactors have been the landlord's ancestors, that does not prove his present utility. The good work of the grandfather is an inadequate apology for the uselessness of the grandson.

Here we touch the prime grievance and kernel of the land question of England, so far as agriculture is concerned. It is felt that the State or community possesses rights with respect to 'economical rent,' and that due satisfaction of these must be reconciled with the proper encouragement and reward of the actual cultivator. Let us first finish considering the claims of the latter.

Can we not effect much which is desirable, and correct not a few anomalies, without breaking with our past and by continuing the ' idea,' to use a Coleridgian expression, of our institutions — by carrying out, not reversing, the history of the tenure of land in England? We can ; and, by studying that past, we shall be encouraged to think that, far from portending some monstrous birth, the throes of agitation touching the land may be the sign of the fulness of time, and that the nation is about to bring forth that which will be neither novel nor appalling. If the student of the history of English land tenures were asked to compress the substance of his researches into small space, doubtless he would reply that from early times until now there has been going on, slowly, with long halts, and some retrogression, a process tending to reduce the number of persons exercising privileges over, and draining revenues from, the soil without discharging functions of commensurate value. The usufructuary and the fructifier tend to be the same ; and the purport of all my past remarks is to prompt the reflection that, if this tendency be continued, there must be great changes, and the purport of all my future remarks is to show in what direction those changes will naturally be. Very many, curious, complicated and onerous, are the tenures which we find in old English law; and their conversion into common socage tenures produced great good to the realm. Blackstone puts the effects before those of Magna Charta itself. So much was then done to strip the tree of the parasitical growth around it. In the history of villeinage, we have, perhaps, a chapter of the same tale. In the villein, it is commonly alleged, though with doubtful accuracy, that we have the predecessor of the copyholder, whose tenure, originally 'base,' and with all the incidents of baseness attaching to it, was in course of time transformed into a tenure differing little in point of value from that of the freeholder. We know that all of these villeins were not manumitted without a struggle. 'We will that ye make us free for ever; ourselves, our heirs, and our lands; and that we be called no more bond, or so reputed. These were the dignified terms in which the peasants, in 1382, made their demands. They were cajoled by empty, false promises. No sooner were they rendered impotent by deceit than the promises which they had received were recalled. There was another chapter of this history completed when tithes were commuted. Though these still remain as a charge on the land, they do not any longer directly touch the cultivator. He no longer only partially gathers the fruits of his labour. Paley, no mean judge, enumerated among the agricultural improvements to be desired in his day, the commutation of tithes, and the enfranchisement of copyholds. The first was accomplished by the act of 1836, and the second is in a fair way to be so. I might also include in the list of such enfranchisements the compulsory sales effected in Ireland, under the Encumbered Estates Act, which relieved Ireland from not a few landlords of the leech species, as well as the more gradual enfranchisement effected by changes in prices, which have often, in process of time, made quit rents insignificant. I might further support the above contention by instances taken from the history of countries such as Prussia and Wurtemburg.[1] But, perhaps, enough of evidence has been collected to corroborate the assertion that the varieties of tenures tend to diminish, and that the *fainéant* landlord tends to disappear.

What, then, is naturally the next phase of this evolution? It appears to me to be this—the enfranchisement of leaseholders ; not turning all farmers at one stroke into landlords, regardless of the rights of the present owners, but the granting of facilities for enfranchisement somewhat similar to those accorded to copyholders. Let all those who are leaseholders [2] be enabled to claim enfranchisement on payment of a sum calculated on the average rent of the last four or five years. Such in substance is one suggestion which I make as a mode of bringing ownership in land more nearly in accordance with the true theory, and as a cure for certain

---

[1] I might here have referred to the Church Estates Act, facilitating the commutation of leases of twenty-one years into estates of fee simple, and the enfranchisement of the tenants of Prince Edward's Island—the former a measure due to Earl Derby, the latter to the late Lord Lytton. The edicts of Stein and Hardenberg in 1807 and 1811 are cases in point.

[2] Or rather, 'all those who are leaseholders or tenants from year to year.'

of the evils which I have catalogued   I shall not answer those who object that this would be a measure of spoliation: a price is to be paid. Neither need I reply to those who say that the above suggestion is Socialism; for, after all, Socialism is nothing other than what the majority of the moment think society should not do, and what the minority of the moment think society should do. But in reply to those who take the more reasonable objection, that there was peculiar ease in commuting copyhold into freehold property, owing to the fact that the dues were determined by custom, it may be stated that the Copyhold Commissioners, in their very first report, complain that they were confronted by the difficulty of determining the value of the ·incidents of copyholds.   Not much greater difficulty, it is submitted, would be encountered in valuing accurately the conflicting claims of lords of the soil and leaseholders.   So many years' purchase of the rack-rent would be the natural basis. No doubt, it will be said, 'If the price is above that which the landlord would obtain in the open market, the suggestion is valueless; if below it, the suggestion is a form of confiscation.' Which is true, if by confiscation is to be understood appropriating all above the average rate of profits—in other words, treating a man no worse than his neighbours. It may be said, too, that the scheme would be practically inoperative. Now, such an assertion conflicts with the experience which we have obtained as to the Irish Land Act. In the working of that act, and particularly in the case of the Marquis of Waterford's estates, we have seen tenants come forward and offer twenty, thirty, and even fifty years' purchase. If such things are done in Ireland, may we not anticipate that more would be done in England, far the wealthier country? Companies would, no doubt, be created to assist in such enfranchisement, even as there have been created companies to assist in enfranchising copyholds; and some might think it worth while to grant to tenants facilities similar to those which are accorded under Bright's clauses. If it be asked what would be the special benefit which would come to pass from such a change, it may be answered that to create, not by violence, but by natural means, not *per saltum*, but gradually, and so much in deference to an ancient tendency as almost plainly to stand justified, a race of proprietors whose domains shall not be so vast as to allow of idleness or indifference to perfect culture, nor so small as to doom them to penury and the necessity of foregoing enterprise or improvements, would not only be the destruction of some of the anomalies which have been mentioned in the early pages of this chapter, but would also establish that state which economists, with few exceptions, have pronounced the most desirable. With large farms and small properties there would be a conjunction of capital with the 'magic of property.' There would be no flagrant instance of the farmer being the sole improver, without sharing in the profits. There would be a splendid object of ambition before the frugal and industrious farmer. The broken rounds in the social ladder which enable one to climb from the lot of the labourer would be mended. The land would, in the language of Wendel Phillips, 'float back into the nation,' and not a little of the dangerous disaffection now rife would vanish.

Meantime, farmers ask for a much smaller boon than the right to become the owners of the soil which they cultivate. They are content to claim greater security of tenure and certain alterations in the law relating to unexhausted improvements, so that they shall not till in peril of their capital or the fruits of their industry being confiscated, and that they may be protected against the risk of being evicted at a six months' notice. Let us consider the condition of the great majority of the farmers of England. It will be seen to be almost incompatible with general high farming. Perhaps, also, it will be held to be at variance with justice. In England leases are rather the exception,[1] and most farms are held on that truly *base* or servile tenure, a yearly tenancy, terminable on six months' notice—a tenure which, I may say, revolts good conscience, and the terms of which most men dare not freely act upon in their dealings with their tenants. ' What is a yearly tenancy?' asks a landlord and the apologist

----

[1] 'An eminent land agent assures me that, out of 1,500 farms which he has let, only one-fourth were on lease.'—Mr. Mechi, May 8, 1871.

of landlords. 'Why, it is an impossible tenure—a tenure which, if its terms were literally interpreted, no Christian man would offer, and none but a madman would accept.'[1] Lord Dufferin has, perhaps, ample warrant for these words. If custom and public opinion, which frowns on the ruthless exercise of the right to evict, did not, so far as it can, punish evictions and mollify this form of tenancy, it might be, as he says, impossible. These checks notwithstanding, the lot of the tenant from year to year is lamentably precarious. At six months' notice he may be turned out of a farm which he and his have cultivated for ages; not in sixteen months, if he be farming well, can he take up all his goods and chattels and effects and depart without loss. If he has put marl or clay upon his farm, the benefits may not be exhausted for fully half a dozen years; the effects of oil-cake, lime, guano, may last for nearly the same period; and if the tenant has erected stone fences, or has drained, it may be a dozen years and more before he is reimbursed. A six months' notice, good enough,

[1] Lord Dufferin, House of Lords, January 14, 1870.

perhaps, when the three-field course of agriculture was general, is somewhat barbarous in these days of high farming.

'Mr. Mechi,' said a sensible farmer, 'has told us to expend 1,000*l.* on every fifty acres. Fancy a man doing this and then being liable to be sent to the right-about by a six months' notice to quit!' He would be a fool or an angel who would farm high in such precarious circumstances. Nor will leases, even of considerable length, secure good farming and the tenant's investments. It is well known that under a nineteen years' lease, such as is the rule in Scotland, a farm is often producing the utmost only for about half the lease. Unless restrained by covenants, an outgoing tenant may 'scourge,' or 'physic' his farm; if he is bound to pursue a certain course of husbandry, he may extract the very utmost consistently with the observance of the letter of the cropping covenants of the lease and immunity from an action for 'waste;' and it may be that he, on entering into possession, found the soil exhausted by his predecessor, tempted like himself to strain the land too much. And so only for a half of the lease may a farm be in good condition. To provide against such contingencies, landowners are wont to append to leases elaborate covenants, binding tenants to follow certain rules of husbandry, e.g., not to take two white grain crops consecutively, not to sell straw, hay, and fodder off a farm, to work it on a three, four, six, or seven years' rotation, to cultivate according to the custom of the country, and to observe it under penalties. When there is no express covenant, it is always assumed that the tenant agrees to follow the custom of the country.[1] But all these precautions shut out one form of evil only to admit another. Men who know their business are told how to do it by men who don't know; or if the cropping covenants are prepared with judgment, they may not, and indeed they

---

[1] 'In the absence of any express covenant on the subject, a covenant or promise is implied on the part of the lessee, that he will use the buildings in a tenantable and proper manner, as that he will manage and cultivate the lands in a good and husbandlike manner, according to the custom of the country; but not that he will make a certain quantity of fallow and spend a certain quantity of manure thereon, and keep the buildings in repair, or any other stipulation not arising out of the bare relation of landlord and tenant.'—Woodfall, *Landlord and Tenant,* p. 123.

cannot, take cognizance of fluctuating circumstances, or favour new scientific methods which it behoves a farmer to watch. Prices may justify his putting a larger stretch under cereals than was contemplated by the framer of the leases. He may see good reason to deviate from 'the custom of the country.' The Leicestershire farmer may desire to abandon the six shift, or 'sair sax,' as it is termed in Scotland, or the five years' course of rotation, the effect of which, to quote the words of a competent authority, resembles 'overdriving a weak horse.'[1] It may happen, too, that the covenants of a lease prevent the sale of straw or stable manures under a heavy penalty, when it would be expedient to purchase more powerful fertilisers. Even when a lease is wisely drawn, and when it is not cunningly framed with an eye to tripping up any tenant who happens to make himself obnoxious, it cannot meet all contingencies; almost inevitably it cramps skill and enterprise; and bound by the covenants of an

[1] A writer in Morton's *Cyclopedia of Agriculture* aptly observes that 'the longest lease passes, during its effluxion, through every variety of short lease, till, at last, it is tantamount to no lease at all.'

ordinary English lease, bristling with minute instructions and penalties, a Jethro Tull or an Albert Thaer might be heavily cast in damages. I may here mention an instance of the mischief which such covenants produce. The scene of the events was the parish of Bourtie in Aberdeenshire. A certain farmer was bound to cultivate according to a seven years' course. Finding that he could not keep a portion of his land clean, he farmed one half under the six years' course and the other under the five years' course. At the end of the lease the farm had been enhanced in value; valuators sent by the owner reported that it had not suffered by the change in cropping. Nevertheless the owner claimed, and claimed with success, a penalty of 30*l.* for a breach of covenant. I shall narrate the upshot in the words of my informant. ' The outgoing tenant was mulcted of his 30*l.*, and had to leave all his improvements, which he had effected by trenching, draining, and making roads and ditches, and the proprietor received about a third more rent from the farm.' I cannot believe that the universal verdict upon this story will be that the tenant quite merited the punishment which he received. There is another evil connected with leases and familiar to all agriculturists. A tenant may farm so well as to farm himself out of his holding. If he has greatly enhanced the letting value of his land, the expiration of his lease may be the signal for a new valuation and a rise in rent. Farming moderately well is safest. The Egyptian fellah tries to look poor to protect himself against the tax-gatherer, and English tenant-farmers are sometimes tempted to take similar precautions against rises of rent. As Allingham in his homely verse says :—

> ' To cut a drain might dig their own pitfall ;
> 'Twere ostentation to rebuild a wall ;
> And did they further dare to stub the whins,
> The great folks soon would visit all their sins.'

Allingham writes of Ireland ; but the same is true of many an English estate. May we not, then, in the light of the absence of leases, of antiquated covenants, or of the danger of an energetic cultivator being rewarded by a rise of rent, say of England, as a whole, that one part of it is farmed by men who dare not improve, owing to insecurity of tenure, and that much of the residue is in the custody of men who are forbidden to farm as well as they could ?·

In some degree these defects are inseparable from leases; and one cannot regard—Scotch agriculturists have long ceased to regard—long leases as the *dernier mot* of agriculture. The same objections which have already been taken to life estates are applicable *à fortiori* to tenancies for a brief term of years. We have seen that the Legislature has been obliged to come to the rescue of the tenant for life, and to bestow upon him not a few of the powers of the owner of the fee simple. And if this step became necessary, notwithstanding the fact that the Common Law gave the tenant for life rights of ownership with respect to emblements, we may ask the Legislature to do as much on behalf of the tenant for a term of years, destitute of any such protection, or, in other words, grant tenant right of some kind to the lessee as well as to the tenant for life. Leases, even if for considerable periods, will not effect the objects enlightened agriculturists have at heart. The greatest of English writers on agriculture has emphatically said, 'I have in different parts of the kingdom seen farms fall in after leases of three lives of the duration of fifty, sixty, and even seventy years, in which the residence of the principal tenant was not to be distinguished from the cottared fields surrounding it.'[1] We want some mode of tenure which will at once keep the tenant in a position of security, which will interest all concerned in the work of reclamation or improvement, and which will prevent those evils incidental to long leases of which Arthur Young speaks.

In his *Gentleman Farmer*—a work which, by the way, contains one of the first rational explanations of the rotation of crops—Lord Kames, struck with the evils incident to leases, and especially with the tenant's temptation to farm badly and 'run out ground' in the last years of his term, proposed that each tenant should receive a lease of nineteen years, with the right of renewal on condition that he paid

---

[1] See Lord Dufferin on *Irish Emigration and the Tenure of Land in Ireland,* and the extracts from the Devon Commission there collected, p. 114.

one-fifth more rent. The landlord was to be
empowered to buy out the occupier on paying ten
years' purchase of the fifth part, or two years' rent.
Lord Kames was before his time: he anticipated the
principle of the Irish Land Act of 1870. Much
less, however, is necessary, it may be thought.
Long leases, with a liberal scale of allowances on
the terms of the Lincolnshire custom, would, it is
said, encourage the tenant to keep his farm in
good condition until the arrival of Lady Day or
Michaelmas on which he was bound to quit, and
would ensure to him remuneration for the marling
of light or fen land, and subsoil draining, or for
improvements which do not yield profit for some
years.   At this point, no doubt, many agriculturists stop in their demands for reform.   They do
not ask compensation for disturbance or eviction.
We cannot, however, be confident that they will
always be so moderate as they are. A demand
for security, if not absolute fixity, of tenure, would
come with force from the mouths of those who
had lived, they and their fathers, on the same
spots time out of mind, who had fertilised the

fields which others may call theirs, and who have
formed indestructible and hallowed associations
therewith. It would be hard to gainsay were
it addressed by farmers of older local standing
than the Hall or Manor family to men whose
rights to rent sprang from mere prescription and
usage, and not from their having mixed their
sweat with the soil. And one hardly knows what
answer could be made to some of those old Warwickshire, Suffolk, or Westmoreland farmers, who
have dwelt for centuries, generation after generation,
in the snug grange; who have seen the lands pass
by accident through a dozen slippery hands; and
who should tell the bailiff of some evictor, the
upstart creature of royal bounty, ' *We* are the old
family; *we* are the persons for whom time has made
a title; *we* are those who should eject if any
should.' What would have been in substance
wrong in the complaints of some of the peasants
whom the Leveson Gowers drove from Sutherland,
or of those who were driven in crowds from
Barra to beg and steal in the streets of Glasgow
and Inverness, had they told their evictors that

they made themselves as good a title as any birth could give? The landlord who has not bought has, at best, but the rights of the oldest tenant. For, in truth, the same causes—formed expectations, associations deeply planted, habits, or, in other words, the fact that the landlord is the oldest tenant—which forbid the confiscation of his estate, even when its genesis was questionable, or openly wicked, sometimes, with almost equal emphasis, condemn evictions. The peasantry or farmers of a district may be the true old county families. Oftentimes they feel towards their cherished farms as an aristocrat does towards the hall of his forefathers. Most of us have known instances in which morally the tenant might turn off the landlord, rather than the landlord the tenant. The long desuetude of a right had created prescription in favour of the latter. England, let us recollect, too, is one of the few countries in which the right to evict freely is claimed. Almost everywhere else there is ' a permanent settlement' of some sort. We give fixity of tenure to the Bengal ryot, under the permanent settlement of 1793. We have given it to the Irish peasantry. Perhaps one day we shall give some such equivalent to the English farmers. Too much seems in the power of one man when he can expel at pleasure those who have dwelt for centuries in the same farm, and who have, really, fertilised it.

Whether there be fixity of tenure or not, some amendment seems necessary in the law relating to fixtures and unexhausted improvements. We have already stated that the legal presumption is that all improvements belong to the landlord. The general rule of law is that ' whenever the tenant has affixed anything to the demised premises, he can never again sever it, without the consent of his landlord.' [1] This rule has been broken down to the advantage of the tenant who erects fixtures for the purpose of trade. In the words of Lord Kenyon, ' In modern times the leaning has been in favour of the tenant, in support of the interests of trade, which has become the pillar of the State.' [2] For reasons barely intelligible, agriculture has not received the full benefit

[1] Woodfall on *Landlord and Tenant*, p. 519.
[2] *Penton* v. *Robsart*, 2 East. 90.

of this relaxation.   An attempt was indeed made to
bestow upon the farmer the right already granted to
the merchant and trader.   But the famous case of
Elwes *v.* Maw put an end to the attempt.   'To give
to the farmer the same facilities which traders had
obtained,' said Lord Ellenborough, 'would introduce a dangerous innovation into the relative state
of rights and interests holden to subsist between
landlord and tenants.'[1]   By statute, indeed, the
tenant is, as we have seen, now at liberty to remove
engines, buildings, &c., erected with the landlord's consent in writing;[2] custom modifies the
Common Law in some half-dozen English counties;
and it is habitual for the in-coming tenant—rarely
the landlord—to pay the out-going tenant for
standing crops, tillage, &c.   But it is still the case
that there exists a legal presumption which does not
lean to the most probable opinion, or in favour of
the weaker party, and that hundreds of thousands
of capital are invested in a manner as unsafe as if
they were vested in the bonds of the craziest of

[1] Smith, L.C., Vol. II.
[2] 14 & 15 Vic. c. 25.

foreign States.[1] Here, too, I must advert to another somewhat questionable privilege which few persons would use for evil purposes, but which have sometimes been employed to the grievous loss of the unwary. If the tenant of the lord of the manor encroaches upon and reclaims a piece of a common or waste, the addition becomes the property of his landlord. For this there is, of course, some manifest reason; but what are we to say to the additional circumstance that, even if the land reclaimed does not belong to the lord of the manor, it is presumed at the end of the tenancy that it is the property of the lessor, and

---

[1] The difference between agriculture and trade in this respect is startling. Mr. Wingrove Cook, in his *Agricultural Tenancies*, cites two surprising cases, *Wyndham* v. *Way*, and *Wordell* v. *Usher* (4 Taunt. 316 and 3 Sco. N. R. 508). ' In the first it was held that a farmer who raises young fruit trees on his farm for the purpose of filling up the orchards is not entitled to sell them. In the second case it was held that a nurseryman who had planted trees in the way of his trade, may remove them, if not of larger growth than could be dealt with in his trade, even though they are producing fruit' (p. 41). Most persons, we presume, will agree with the opinion of Mr. Pusey's Committee, that ' this distinction does not appear to be supported by any sound reason,' and that ' the tenant's privilege of removal with respect to fixtures set up for trading purposes, should be extended to those erected for agricultural purposes.'

that in the absence of proof that the new field was not included in the lease, the landlord may take it and all that has been expended upon it?   'The tenant steals for the benefit of the landlord'—such seems substantially the Common Law, Lord Campbell's protest against this pithy maxim to the contrary notwithstanding.   We need scarcely observe that an exasperated lord of the manor might turn this presumption into an engine of cruelty towards the labourers who have been suffered to squat on the edges of many an English common.   An actual instance will reveal many disagreeable possibilities. A labourer in Cardiganshire reclaimed a piece of land from the common of Penarth.   He then sold it for 4*l.* 10*s.* to a kinsman, Davies, a neighbouring farmer.   But by-and-by the Earl of Lisburne, lord of the manor, came on the scene ; the purchaser was turned out ; and the Earl, we presume, still enjoys the field of Cae Rhos,[1] to which another had imparted all its value.

Modus et conventio vincunt legem, it will be said ;

----

[1] *Earl of Lisburne* v. *Davies*, I. L.R.C.P., 259.   See also *Andrew* v. *Hailes*, 2 E. & B. 353.

and it may be alleged that farmers have it in their power to obtain security by bargaining for it and by declining to accept leases from which covenants for compensation for unexhausted improvements are absent. But this blinks the fact that the majority of farmers are refused leases, and that they must, up to certain limits, assent to the terms which the landowner proposes. The notion that they are a class possessed of capital which they can or will employ elsewhere the moment their gains in agriculture fall below the average current return on capital, is a favourite fiction with those who have studied and have not too well understood the writings of economists. The ordinary tenant-farmer must get a holding, if for no other reason than that he would sacrifice his skill were he to quit his vocation. He does not bargain at arm's length with his landlord. How, too, could it be otherwise considering the power of the latter to accept with comparative safety tenants destitute of means, and thus to create a fictitious competition for farms? The law of distraint in England, and that of hypothec in Scotland, give the landlord a preference over all other creditors, and enable him to admit a class of persons who are prepared to submit to any conditions however rigorous. In such circumstances the landowner may receive more than ' economical rent.' [1]

To alter the legal presumption with respect to fixtures and unexhausted improvements, or to declare that the custom—say of Lincolnshire—should be legalised and should be in force, whenever the contrary is not agreed upon, would probably be found insufficient, though one cannot forget that the custom made the ungenial Lincoln soil, in Arthur Young's opinion, ' the garden of England.' If landowners were disposed to suffer their tenants to improve freely, and to ensure compensation, it would be unnecessary to alter the existing law ; if the law were altered, there is no reason to believe that their present disposition would change. ' Can we expect

---

[1] ' Continued enactments were passed up to 1 & 2 Philip and Mary, c. 12, for the protection of tenants ; but as the independence and power of tenants in opposition to their landlords increased, the current of legislative enactments took a turn and has ever since been for the benefit and advantage of landlords.'—Woodfall's *Landlord and Tenant*, p. 374.

the very men who now refuse to give their tenants
the shortest lease, to be found cheerfully to assent
to their acquiring something like a permanent
interest by the improvement of their farms?'[1]
Would not the insertion of a few more words in
every lease be the net result of the change? At
most, would not the benefit produced by legalising
the tenant-right customs of the country be confined
to the general introduction of leases and of a power
to bind the remainder man to remunerate a tenant
for *bonâ fide* improvements? Failing to discern
any very good reason for endowing the owner with
a patent to repress improvements, I humbly submit that the Legislature cannot well stop short of
endowing the tenant with certainty that if he add
to the value of his holding in any appreciable
degree he will be sure to acquire a lien over, or interest in, the land to that amount. If he injures
his farm—if, to quote the expressive phrase of the
Code Napoléon,[2] he fails to cultivate it *en bon père*

---

[1] *The Irish People and the Irish Land.* By Isaac Butt,
p. 227.

[2] Code civil, liv. iii. 1766.

M

de famille—let him make good the damage, dila-
pidation, or waste; if, on the other hand, he
enhances the value, let his be all the gain. If the
value which he adds to the estate be 5*s.* an acre,
let him rank as a creditor against the estate to that
amount. The landlord would receive back his land
as valuable as when he leased it, and the farmer
would be encouraged to treat his farm as tenderly
and wisely as if it were his own. Such seems the
simple mode in which men of wealth would be
induced to cultivate scientifically, and in which
dependent tenants would be protected; and such
also seems to me the simple mode in which the
tenant farmers might work out the enfranchisement
of which we have spoken. Not so much leases, as
the power to realise whatever value one has added
to the soil, and the liability to make good what one
has subtracted, speaking generally, ' the tenant's
license to improve,' with the landlord's right of set
off—such seem, then, the lines of reform; and
though there is obviously much practical friction
to be overcome in executing such a reform—though
the employment of valuators, or a 'court, opens a

wide door for dissatisfaction—it might not be found to be incapable of realisation. The proposal is made with a profound sense of the impotence of valuators.[1] But permissive registration of improvements might facilitate the task ; and, failing all other machinery, the valuation might be the rent which the farm fetched in market overt—not, indeed, a perfect test of the monetary worth of the unexhausted improvements, but one not necessarily more favourable to the tenant than to the landlord. As to the objection that any fine to be paid by the incoming tenant is a serious hindrance to him, and an onerous subtraction from his capital, it is, after all, a portion of the rent : and it seems highly unnecessary, and even inexpedient, that the whole fine should be paid at once. True, in Ulster, where these recommendations are practically in force, not unfrequently, the tenant enters into possession after having paid a sum which makes him poor and incapable of working his farm; but it does not appear why the fine or grassum should be forthcoming

---

[1] Lord Dufferin on *Emigration and the Tenure of Land in Ireland*, p. 241.

at once any more than are all the instalments of rent.[1]   Only, then, give the tenant power to add to the value of the soil by his own skill as much as he chooses, and one will in course of time behold an easily and admirably working system—the tenant obtaining the position of a proprietor, provided he be industrious and skilful ; the tenant for all good work recouped either by the landlord or by the incoming tenant.   Only let that system be in operation for some time, and the enfranchisement of the soil, a matter of difficulty when regarded as a bargain with money paid down, seems more easy and practicable, for it is seen that the tenant may work out his freedom.[2]

To show how the existing law relative to improvements operates for evil, let me narrate one or two plain tales.   The first relates to the transactions of a leading evangelical nobleman, whose

---

[1] In Guernsey it is very common for the purchaser of an estate to pay for it by perpetual corn rents, or by a payment of one-fourth in money and a conversion of the remainder into corn rents.—Duncan's *History of Guernsey*, p. 286.

[2] What is above suggested is, substantially, the law of Denmark.—*Reports on Tenure of Land Abroad*, Part i. p. 192.

estates lie in a northern county. About the year 1848 a farm labourer was allowed by 'the ground officer' or steward, to build a house and improve a barren piece of land. With the aid of his neighbours, he brought under cultivation about ten acres. No lease was stipulated for; no rent was charged; the land was loosely connected with an adjoining farm; and it is believed that no entry of this 'croft' was made in the books of the estate. By-and-by, it was sold to a nobleman whom I need not name. His commissioner, in course of time, discovered this unnoted plot; and the 'crofter' received notice that he must immediately pay '10*l.* for the bygone crop, 10*l.* for the crop in the stackyard, 10*l.* for the crop about to be laid down, and 10*l.* annually for a nineteen years' lease of the croft.' The labourer could not accede to these terms; he was turned out; the vacant land was advertised and let for 14*l.* a year; and, to use my informant's blunt words, 'the Earl pockets this sum, and the crofter lives again on his days' wages.' In the district where these events took place, land sells for thirty years' purchase, and is bought to yield about 3 per cent.

Assuming that the value of this croft did not enter into the price of the estate, we find that the Earl appropriated 420*l.* morally earned by a labourer. The second instance of legal spoliation which I shall mention relates to estates situated at no great distance from the scene of the former tale. A tenant entered into possession of a small farm of fifty to sixty acres. He died before he obtained a lease, leaving a widow and a young son. Not being able to furnish due security, she was refused a lease ; but on the faith of a verbal promise from the trustees of the estate, she and her son reclaimed about thirty acres of barren land in the course of fifteen years, and during that time obtained no profit. But two neighbouring farmers coveted the little spot won from the wilderness, and she was informed that she must quit her holding. She presented vouchers showing that she had expended 96*l.* on manures during the four preceding years, and 32*l.* for trenching and draining during the two preceding years ; for these items, at all events, she pleaded for compensation ; the outlay of the past years might go for nothing, but these expenses were of recent date. She was denied all compensation ; she had presumed to take legal advice on the subject; she must suffer. So 'the widow and her son were turned adrift, and found another farm on the banks of the Waitna, in New Zealand.' A third instance occurs to me : the particulars are derived from the lips of the chief sufferer. R—— E—— became the tenant of the farm of T——, at Whitsunday in the year 1853. The farm consisted of 150 acres of arable land, together with a considerable amount of improvable land. The rent was 150*l.*; and to the outgoing tenant, ten years of whose lease were unexpired, he paid a grassum or fine of 700*l.* Shortly after entering the farm, he obtained a new lease of nineteen years, and he covenanted to improve thirty acres of bog, and five acres of woodland, as well as to drain a certain portion. In 1862 he died. His widow, Mrs. E——, was not heir-at-law, and the heir-at-law was too poor to step into his shoes. Accordingly the farm, thus enormously enhanced in value, fell into the hands of the landlord. R—— E—— had entered into the farm with a capital of 2,000*l.*, and he had expended 1,000*l.* on its improvement. When the estate was wound up, there remained to the widow a balance of 63*l.* The next instance which I shall cite is taken from the annals of the same parish, and a widow was again the sufferer. M——, tenant of the farm of K——, expended upwards of 12,000*l.* in building houses, draining, fencing, and in conducting water from some distance to drive a threshing mill. It appears that he was warned by his friends of the imprudent nature of his investment; but the warm assurance of the proprietor encouraged the tenant, who could not believe that he would ever be evicted from a farm where he and his ancestors had lived for nearly a century. When M—— died, his widow requested a renewal of the tenancy from the new proprietor, a tenant for life. She was told that no offer from her would be received; and she was ousted from the farm. Let me mention one more simple tale of many which I have heard, and again I take it from the same district. J—— M——, an old man in needy circumstances, was in danger of being cast on the parish. Some kind friends came to his aid. A proprietor gave a 'stance' or site, the old man's neighbours carted the requisite stones, and the Kirk Session furnished so much money. A few years after the house was built, M——'s eldest son obtained a lease of ten acres of hill side on condition that he should bring them under cultivation, and he should pay a moderate increase of rent at the expiration of the lease. On the strength of this bargain, he worked industriously; he built a barn and a byre; and he looked forward, no doubt, to spending his days on the little farm which he had reclaimed. A new proprietor had succeeded to the estate before the lease expired, and on its running out notice was given that the rent would be raised from 30s. to 8l. Such a rent he could not pay; and so he departed, leaving the reclaimed land and the houses to the lord of the soil. True, if the injured man could derive comfort from the thought that others had fared as ill as he, he might enjoy that comfort, for a neighbouring crofter, who had reclaimed from the bog and heather eight acres of land, and who had built houses thereon, was also evicted. These samples, taken from a limited area, need no ample comment. Legal though they were, they were akin to the principles of Macheath. Rich and respected some of these landlords are; but 'the spoil of the poor is in your houses,' notwithstanding.

Though agricultural rent is less of the character of economical rent than the ground rent in cities, it is partially the price of inherent qualities; and of it also we may ask, Are we to suffer it to be monopolised by private persons? Now, we have already stated some reasons why the purchase of the entire soil would be inexpedient. There are, however, some modes of partially acquiring the right to 'economical rent,' and among them is the proposal of Mr. Mill, that the State should appropriate, either wholly or partially, the future spontaneous increases of rent. 'From the present date,' he says, 'or at any subsequent time at which the Legislature may think fit to assert the principle, I see no objection to declaring that the future increment of rent should be liable to special taxation, in doing which all injustice to the landowners would be obviated, if the present market value of the

land were secured to them ; since that includes the
present value of all future expectations.' To the
direction of this suggestion there seems no valid
objection, if the above exposition of principles be
true. But it may be said, on the one hand, that
the proposal falls short of the premises ; they warrant the complete absorption of economical rent ;
Mr. Mill would appropriate only a part. Further,
the suggestion would be more valuable were it accompanied by directions as to how ' increase of rent
from natural causes ' can be discriminated from the
rises ascribable to a landowner like the Marquis of
Tweeddale, or a skilful industrious tenant, and how
such special taxation could be made compatible
with the existence of due encouragement to improve. Excellent in some respects, commendable
in particular by reason of its simplicity, it seems to
err in at once taking too much and too little—too
little because it leaves uncorrected what is now
wrong, too much because it would sometimes absorb the interest of capital, and would discourage
new investments in the improvement of land.

The objections which have already been taken

to the complete purchase of land by the State are applicable to the case of agricultural land. Its value twenty or thirty years hence is so uncertain that the amount of compensation now awarded, were the fee simple or reversion bought, might for ever make the bargain unremunerative. But, of course, if there were reasonable prospects of a rapid increase of value, it might be advantageous to resort to the purchase of remote reversionary interests. At the same time, there is small probability of such an idea being ever carried into effect; and in these circumstances, I revert to another of the expedients mentioned in the second chapter—to impose a slight addition to the present land tax, or allow no tax or rate on real property of ancient date to be removed. Perhaps these expedients, and especially the latter, in the event of the expenditure of the State diminishing, would prove efficacious.

I sum up : The tenant to be permitted to add whatever value to the land he pleases, and a sub-tenant to be permitted to do the same ; the difference in value to go to the outgoing tenant, and to be paid by the incoming tenant or landlord, in a lump sum or by instalments, ' payment prompt,' or payment deferred. So far the tenant, thus enabled to work himself into a proprietorial position. On the other hand, the State at long intervals to add slightly to the land tax, to retain whatever imposts on realty are of old date, and to purchase present or reversionary interests wherever or whenever such a course is deemed expedient.

CHAPTER VI.

PROPERTY IN MINES.

ANOMALOUS as is our land tenure, both in cities and in the country, vast and indefensible as are the privileges of the lord of the soil, these anomalies and these privileges do not surpass, and perhaps do not equal, those which exist with respect to mines. Here we stand alone.   We govern mines as no other nation does.   We lavish on the owner of the fee simple rights such as his social equivalent nowhere else enjoys over the minerals that lie below his estate.   *Ab cœlo usque ad centrum terræ—* all, with a paltry exception, is his.   The earth is the landlord's and the fulness thereof; the luck of the discoverer is his too ; the progress of mineralogical science enriches him; and the labour of geologists and the results of government surveys, and local skill with regard to the run of ' lodes ' and faults, go to swell the rental of the landlord. Yet how few of those who treat of the land question and blame our system of land tenure, bestow more than a passing word on this, its weakest, and certainly its most singular, part. While there appear books, articles, pamphlets and addresses by the score, denouncing our land laws, so far as they relate to farming, I can scarcely recall one writer who has taken the trouble to show that there is anything very wrong in our mining laws. And yet not only is there very much to be amended—not only is 'economical rent' absorbed by private proprietors—but it is possible to put mining property on a sound basis without trampling on numerous private interests and without its being necessary to compensate at every step in the path of reform. Here, and here alone, our hands are free to do that which reflection counsels. Here there is wealth which no man has yet appropriated. That state of nature, of which Rousseau tells us when the earth was common and unappropriated, is no dream; it exists—it lies beneath our feet. But each day a new appropriation is made; that species of territorial conquest or occupation which we are wont to associate only with rude or primitive times, is repeated to-day in England. We have curtailed the squatter's liberty in Australia, in New Zealand, and indeed, in all our colonies. But the squatter's right over domains which are worth perhaps as much as the fee simple of our Colonial Empire, is still part and parcel of the law of England, which each day tolerates not merely the continuance of the outcome of a vicious system but also sanctions new applications of it.

According to the English law, all minerals and quarries, with the exception of gold and silver, belong to the owner of the fee simple. The State has no right to them. The discoverer has none. The owner of the fee simple carries away everything. He may work the minerals on his estate as he pleases. He may waste them, he may forbid others working them. There is no royalty or special tax to be paid by him. The few exceptions to all this liberty are not of much consequence; but I may recite them. Though the Crown claims all gold and silver mines, wherever discovered, this Com-

mon Law privilege has been made almost worthless
by an enactment—the 5 William and Mary, c. 6—
which declared that no copper, tin, iron, or lead
mines should be regarded as royal mines, even
though gold or silver was found therein, but which
added that the Crown would have the right of pre-
emption of the ore when on bank, at certain prices
—16*l.* a ton for copper, tin 40*s.*, iron 40*s.*, and
lead 9*l.* I recite these figures because they illustrate the neglect of the revenues of the Crown.
Had its original powers at Common Law been
retained, the State would now be drawing a handsome revenue from the lead mines, especially those
of Cumberland and Devonshire, which in 1870
yielded silver of the value of 196,140*l.* 9*l.* a ton
for lead ore would have left a handsome margin.
Unfortunately, in the reign of George III., the
owners, taking alarm at the high prices paid for
lead during the French war, induced Parliament to
alter the scale to 25*l.*, and destroy the rights of the
Crown.[1] The Crown is also the owner of minerals

[1] Mr. Bainbridge, in his treatise on ' The Law of Mines and
Minerals,' points out that it is quite possible for the prices of

found below the sea and up to high-water mark.
But this privilege has not yet been found to be
of much worth. So far the rights of the Crown,
which somewhat curtail the doctrine of the Common Law. I ought to mention as another exception the special legislation which governs the mines
of the Dean Forest, as well as those of Cornwall
and Devonshire. In these cases there is recognition
of the discoverer's right. In the Dean Forest, part
of the Crown demesnes, there have grown up various
customs with respect to the ownership of the minerals. Some of the inhabitants of the Forest and
of the Hundred of St. Briavels, calling themselves
'free miners,' claimed of old the right to search
for and work minerals within those domains. An
Act of Parliament, passed in the beginning of the
present reign, recognised that right, and laid down

rich and peculiar iron ores like red hæmatite to rise above
the sum fixed for pre-emption, that the value of some copper
ores is now much above the sum fixed by 5 Will. & Mary, c. 6,
and that, ' in general, the sum fixed for tin ore would be
greatly inadequate.' 'It follows, therefore, that if it could
be proved that any of the ores just mentioned contained any
portion of gold or silver, the Crown would have the right of
pre-emption at a price which might still seriously affect the
interests of the producer.'—Bainbridge, 3rd edit. p. 62.

rules conceived in the spirit of the local customs.[1] All persons who had laboured a year and a day in a coal or iron mine in the Hundred were held to be entitled to the privileges of 'free miners.' As such they were empowered to receive leases from the Crown Commissioners. They acquired an interest of 'the nature of real estate,' conditional on their faithfully paying certain rents or royalties to the Crown. As to the Cornwall tin mines, it was formerly essential that all tin extracted therefrom should be coined into blocks of 320 lbs. each, and that a certain royalty thereon should be paid to the Prince of Wales of the day. This obligation was abolished by the 1 and 2 Vic. c. 120; and such portions of the Prince of Wales' revenue as were formerly derivable from that source were made a charge on the Consolidated Fund. At the same time, also, the Customs duty on tin and tin ore was reduced. Next session of Parliament, however, there was passed an Act, calling attention to the privileges granted by this legislation to the tinners of Cornwall, who were exempted from dues paid by the copper

---

[1] 1 & 2 Vic. c. 43, amended by 24 & 25 Vic. c. 40.

miners, and imposing a duty of one farthing a ton
on tin and tin ore.   No account of the mining law
in force in Cornwall could omit reference to the
custom of 'bounding.'   It is in curious variance
with English ideas respecting the sacredness of property.   It is still the case that anyone may go on
waste land, or land once waste and subject to the
custom, mark off a certain area, appropriate it,
unless the bounder's right is challenged by some
prior occupier, and work it on condition that there
is paid a 'toll tin,' varying from one-tenth to one-
fifteenth of the produce.   In the mining customs in
force in Derbyshire, there is also recognition of the
right of the discoverer.   By the local customs, now
confirmed and defined by Acts of Parliament, the
'free miner' who discovers a vein of lead is entitled to two 'meers;' a 'meer' being a space of
twenty-seven to thirty-two yards in length in a
'rake' vein, and of fourteen square yards in flat
or pipe mining.   The lord of the soil is a secondary
person; he receives only one 'meer' for the whole
vein.

Thus there exist in the oldest mining districts—

for such are Cornwall and the Dean Forest—local laws which recognise at once the claims of the State and the discoverer. But the Common Law, which governs the bulk of mining property, heeds neither. To the owner of the fee simple it gives everything. This doctrine was carried with the rest of our laws to the United States; but it has been deemed proper to alter it by statute in some of the States—in that of New York, for instance.[1] In truth, when the Englishman goes abroad to colonise, he does not carry with him his superstitious feeling of respect for the landowner. He subjects it to critical examination. He owns that the State and the discoverer have their due claims over minerals. In Australia it has been customary to introduce into deeds of grant of land from the Crown clauses reserving the minerals. There, miners have ridden rough-shod over the so-called rights of property, and when the proprietors themselves are not engaged in working some vein, their neighbours have sometimes followed up their pursuit of gold or silver, careless whither they went, and even continued the

[1] Kent, vol. iii. p. 483.

search below streets, churches, and cemeteries. In Victoria the Government have lately introduced a bill which seems to give ample encouragement to the miner.   The proprietor of the surface is promised the right of pre-emption of a mining lease ; but if he declines to accept, the right will fall to persons ready to mine and willing to give securities for damages that may happen to be done to buildings or the surface.[1]   Only in England, or rather in certain parts of it, do we see the State and the discoverer pushed aside and ignored.

Certainly on the Continent all is different ; and those who contrast our land tenure with that of France and Germany, for example, do not point the sharp contrast as clearly as they might if they forget to mention the antagonism of our laws governing mines to those which are in force abroad. There the State occupies the lucrative place which we assign to the freeholders.   More or less also the discoverer's claim to consideration is, as a rule, recognised abroad.   The Civil Law has had much to do with the notions of mining property which

---

[1] *Times*, October 1, 1872.

have become supreme on the Continent. On this subject the Roman Law spoke variously and uncertainly. At some times the Emperors put forth pretensions to all minerals. At other times their demands fell far short of this. I borrow from Mr. Rogers' work on Mines the following account of the mining law in force at Rome: 'Under the Civil Law, in its purest times, gold, silver, and other precious metals usually belonged to the State, whilst all other minerals, mines, and quarries belonged to the owner of the soil, subject in some cases to a partial, and in others to a more general, control of the fiscus.' Towards the end of feudal times, in both France and Germany, the right of the sovereign to all minerals was asserted. Sully believed the mines of France to be the estate of his royal master. It was not until the approach of the Revolution that other ideas began to be mooted. Turgot brought his supreme sagacity to bear on the question of the true nature of mining property, which was becoming a problem of interest in his days; and his tract or memoir, ' *Des Mines et des Carrières*,' disfigured though it is by several fallacies, is admirably concise, luminous, and acute.   In the capacity of *Intendant* of Limoges, he wrote, on the occasion of the application of certain companies to be allowed to work the lead mines of Glanges, Haute Vienne, this memoir, which is not only a criticism of the law then in operation, the *droit régalien*, but which is also by anticipation an assault on the mining code which was subsequently enacted in France.   He starts from the principle that the man who owns the surface owns what is below, minerals and all, and proceeds to argue thus : ' The whole of the surface is his property, there is no denying; therefore, no one can without his consent break ground thereon.'   Yet Turgot, apparently so far a friend of a mining law in principle like ours, goes on to maintain that the proprietor of the surface ought not to be empowered to hinder one who has sunk a shaft or pit in another man's land from driving a gallery below his estate in pursuit of a seam or vein.   His reasons, which will be familiar to colonists who never heard Turgot's name, but which will jar with English notions respecting real property, we quote ; and they are these : ' First, because occu-

pation has not descended so deep ; second, because
the considerations of equity and common interest,
which have made society guarantee to the first cultivators the fruit of their labours, have no application
to what is underground, which is neither an object
of cultivation nor the produce of labour ; third, because the proprietor suffers no harm or annoyance
when openings are not made in his estate ; fourth,
because a little after property in land was established society itself had not the means of enforcing
this legal guarantee of the possession of minerals.'
It will be at once said that these reasons, if good for
anything, are fatal to the pretensions of the proprietor of the soil to property in the unextracted
ore ; and in truth Turgot admits as much.   He
distinctly affirms that until minerals are extracted or
appropriated, they are nobody's, and that they
belong to the proprietor of the surface only if he
has spent labour or its worth upon them.   Not all
mineral wealth, but merely the right of saying who
shall break ground, is, in Turgot's opinion, the
accessory of the fee simple.   This memoir was not
fired off in the air.   In 1791 the question came

for decision before the National Assembly; and Turgot's arguments were discussed with heat, and challenged by Mirabeau among others. In his fierce, contemptuous way, he dismissed Turgot's proposal for free mining with the remark that 'it would make our mines an inextricable labyrinth, and that this sort of conquest going on in the middle of society, would leave mines to the rule of chance.' Mirabeau declared that they should be at 'the disposal of the nation;' meaning thereby that the State should see that they were worked, and that wisely and well. And Mirabeau carried the day; for such was the substance of the law passed in July 1791. Then came a change. The principle advocated by Mirabeau seemed to be effaced by the Civil Code, one of the articles of which laid it down that 'the property of the surface carries with it property in all below.' Again, in 1810, the much-vexed question came up, and, in spite of Napoleon's fondness for a law somewhat similar to that of England, there was passed an enactment, still in force, putting the State in its old place, and restoring the *droit régalien.* Of the three categories, *mines*, *minières*, and *carrières*, it was declared that the first could be worked only on a concession or lease from the State being granted. The *concessionnaire* or lessee must pay a fixed rent of 10 francs the square *kilomètre*, and also a percentage on the ' output.' *Minières*, the term used to describe alluvial deposits of metal, such as the peroxide of iron one gets in the tin washings of Cornwall, belong to the proprietor of the soil; but they cannot be worked without the permission of the Government. Only quarries may be worked freely by the owner of the soil. I may add that he has no preferential claim to the concession of a mine situated on his own estate. I have spoken rather fully of the law of France because its leading principles have been adopted elsewhere. It is in force in Belgium, except in the provinces of Hainault, Liege, and Limbourg. In Germany there is ample recognition of the right of the State. In Prussia the mines are the property of the nation, and they can be worked only on a concession being granted, and subject to the surveillance of the State.[1]

[1] See the weak side of the Prussian mining system, pointed

There is some consideration shown in Germany to the claims of the discoverer or adventurer. The local adages *Es hat jederman ein freyes Schürfen* and *Der erste Finder ist der erste Muther* bear witness to this fact. In Austria, Italy, and Spain, the mines belong to the State, and are let on leases. Only in Russia do we meet with a law which seems at first blush to invest the landowner with ample powers, equal to those with which the English freeholder is gifted. But on closer inspection we find that it is not so, and that the Russian noble does not stand in the enviable position of the English proprietor of an estate on the coal measures or above the iron-stone of South Staffordshire. Most of the Russian mines, such as those in the Ural Mountains, are situated in the vast Crown domains; and, moreover, the State not only claims the right to sell the produce of mines, Crown or private, but it also imposes a heavy tax on all ore. Certainly, then, not in Russia

out in Banfield's *Manufactures of the Rhine*, p. 55. None of them are necessarily connected with the proposals here advocated. If royalties are charges varying according to the gross amount of ore produced, of course, mines badly situated or naturally unproductive must be unfairly taxed.

can we procure a precedent for our manner of dealing with mineral property.

To the mere circumstance that we are almost solitary, and that our law is nearly unique, one cannot attach much consequence; and, armed with sufficient reasons in the background, one need not rest one's case on the basis of authority, even though that authority be the conspiring testimony of almost all nations and ages. Justifications of the rights of property, in land or movables, may be reduced to three. I have taken the trouble to look into various writers on the subject, such as Locke, and, in later times, Troplong, Thiers, and Faucher. Some of those apologists of property cited only two justifications, but none cited more than three—the justice or expediency of giving to a man absolute control over that on which he has expended toil, thought, or capital; the right which is acquired by first occupancy; and that which is created by prescription or undisturbed possession for a long period. I accept these criteria of what ought to be a man's property; I apply them to the privileges showered on the English landowner; and I venture to submit that these justifications do not cover the ample extent of his prerogatives, appropriating as he does that on which no man has expended a fraction of labour or wealth, which he has never seen, far less occupied, and about which no right of prescription could have grown up. Of course, it is questionable how far prior occupation, one of the so-called natural modes of acquisition, deserves to create a title in a civilised state of society. It may suit barbarous and sparsely-peopled countries; but it seems being guided by names and not reasons to apply in a populous society the doctrines of the Civilians with respect to occupation to waste land of vast extent or mineral property of great value. When a person claims, in virtue of first occupation, some rich vein of metal, irresistibly we think of Adrian IV. granting, as ' king of all islands,' the lordship of Ireland, or some monarch claiming as his own half a continent because his flag had first waved there.

But, accepting all these three modes of acquisition as valid in equity, we may point out—and it is almost needless to prove—that none of them warrant the appropriation of mineral deposits which are unexpectedly discovered. Let us see whether this is so, and whether it is fraught with consequences of moment. Mr. Godwin Austen and Mr. Prestwich assure us that they are confident that coal can be got at workable depths in the valley of the Thames. There is a coal-trough running from Belgium across the sea, along the Thames, by Bristol, and extending into Ireland; and shafts some hundreds of feet deep would probably, according to the latter geologist, bring us to the coal measures. The opinion was controverted by Sir Roderick Murchison; but Mr. Prestwich has collected no small amount of proofs, both from geological and palæontological considerations, that a huge coal basin is continued below the Thames. There is a possibility that experimental borings may substantiate his surmises; and if they prove true, the discovered coal will at once accrue to the landowners beneath whose estates it happens to lie. Now, could one say that they had expended labour or capital on coal, the very existence of which was unknown and even unsuspected until Mr. Godwin Austen and Mr. Prestwich threw out the idea? If such coal exist, it did

not form an element in determining the purchase
money of the overlying soil, if it ever was purchased.   Prior occupation is out of the question,
for no man could occupy that which no man had
dreamt of.   There could not be the *affectus occu-
pandi* with respect to what the mind could not
fasten upon.   And as for the right of prescription,
its basis is the fact that it is wrong to allow a man
to act as owner for the space of twenty or forty
years and then to eject him.   But what expectations could be defeated when none could be
formed, and how could prescription be ripening
when possession did not exist?   As Napoleon observed, with his wonted trenchant sagacity, ' The
discovery of a mine creates a new property ; an act
of the sovereign becomes necessary.'   In the presence of such a discovery, the community is free
to act as seems good to it ; no vested rights, sacred
in the eye of morality, stay its hands ; and if Parliament were to pass a law to the effect that all new
deposits, veins, and seams of minerals discovered in
the United Kingdom after 1873 should belong to
the State, there would be no injustice to complain

of, and no good reason in the world for demanding compensation. Certainly no jurist could find fault with such a measure were twenty years of grace allowed.

I next apply the touchstone of the three customary justifications of the rights of property to minerals the position of which is known, but which are not worked owing to their depth or the inadequate price of ore; and it seems to me that none of them is broad enough to cover the English landowner's ample privileges. The Royal Commission which reported in 1871 on the subject of our coal supply assume that shafts may one day be profitably carried down four thousand feet, a depth at which it is now impossible to work, owing to the increase of temperature as one descends into the bowels of the earth. At present, minerals lying more than three thousand feet below the surface are practically unworkable. They will sell for nothing; they will be worth nothing for many a day, until the art of mining is much improved or prices rise much above their present position; and if the State appropriated the unworked, and for the

o

time unworkable, deposits, in view of the possibility
or probability of their being ultimately in request,
it would not be bound in equity to compensate
the owners.   Unbought and untouched by capital
or labour, they are still no man's property.   Appropriated or occupied they cannot be said to be:
as well might one say that one had occupied the
moon by often thinking about it or looking at it, as
assert that one had occupied the coal that lies six
hundred fathoms down, below the tertiary rocks.
And as for the rights which prescription, use, and
habit create, they do not seem to apply reasonably
to the case before us.   One can understand prescription when it means that a man should be allowed
to continue to use that which he habitually has
used ; but it sounds nonsensical to speak of a prescriptive right to what one never saw, never used,
and perhaps never dreamt of using.   If, therefore,
the State were to declare public property the 56,273
millions of tons of coal which, we are told, lie
under rocks newer than the coal measures, and such
portions of the coal measures as have not yet been
worked, or if it were to say that the ironstones

which may be hereafter found in formations similar to the Cleveland Hill seams should belong to the State, there would be no good grounds for listening to demands for compensation. At all events, it would be possible to guard against all inconvenience and hardship by allowing the landowner to work as much and as freely as he liked during the next twenty years.

We pass now to those mines which are already in operation. In these, with their shafts, and galleries, and buttresses, and engines, millions of capital have been sunk. There true rights of property exist. Only let us, while conceding this, not admit too much. Of course, as a rule, the person who has put himself to all the outlay is one who is content with a lease for a term of years; but making the most favourable assumption for the landowner, that he works as well as owns a mine, has he acquired a right to go on working some particular strata indefinitely? No, seems the right answer. He has a title, good in point of equity, to get a fair return on his capital and labour; and if Parliament interposes before he has done so, and intercepts his probable profits, Parliament ought to make good his unexpected losses. But the right of prior occupation and prescription surely do not go further. It is one thing for a man to claim a spot of land for himself and his successors for all time, and quite another to claim for all time the liberty to make a fresh appropriation every day. It is the latter claim—a prescriptive right to add to his estate—which the owner of the minerals puts forward, and he cannot fence it round with reasons which compass only the former. The latter claim corresponds not to the comparatively modest pretensions of the landowner in a civilised community, satisfied with remaining where he is, but rather to those of the squatter, who will to-day be here, and to-morrow will drive his flocks onwards; and if we have curtailed his license to roam on, appropriating in his march all that is unoccupied, there is surely much to be said in favour of no longer declaring that that is sound policy and justice if done perpendicularly, which is waste and usurpation when done laterally. I find that Turgot anticipates and confirms much of what I deferentially urge: 'Celui qui a pris la matière sur dix toises de longueur n'a pas plus de droit sur la suite de ce filon jusqu'à cent et jusqu'à mille toises plus loin, que le propriétaire de la surface n'en avait sur la totalité.' It is a mere fallacy to contend that one has acquired a right to the end of a seam because one has appropriated the beginning. He who challenges the justice of the landowner's claim to be permitted to go on working indefinitely any mine or to be compensated if he is stopped at any stage, finds fault with the new applications of an old system : the former would not, of necessity, take away what is already appropriated.

Some may think that the discoverer of mines is more worthy of reward than either the landowner or the community ; and such as are of that mind must be shocked by our Common Law, which ignores altogether the discoverer. The ' old men,' the cunning miners skilled in ' shodding,' the village geologist who identifies some stratum with that in a neighbouring field, and so leads to the finding of a valuable deposit, receive nothing. How vast have been the accessions to rent rolls from sudden discoveries of minerals, for which proprietors can claim no credit! Let me quote what Mr. Mushet, the first to recognise the worth of the ' black band ' or carbonaceous ironstone which goes in Lanarkshire by his name, says of the results which took place after 1801 : 'The estate of Airdrie now returns to the proprietor, for royalty on black band discovered by me in 1801, 12,000*l.* a year ; whereas formerly not one shilling of mineral rent was obtained.' What estimate is too large of the accession to the rentals of the landowners of South Staffordshire after Mr. Thorncycroft of Wolverhampton proved the value of the ironstone of the district! Not twenty years ago the demands on the South Staffordshire iron beds led to the opening up of the Cleveland Hills, the enormous wealth of which had been before ignored.

I would add that it is not merely casual services of which the landowners have reaped the benefit. The State has assisted them directly. For many years there has been going on a geological survey carried out at the public cost. Skilled men of science have been employed. Each year a report on one or more counties, drawn up by Mr. Juke, Mr. Egerton, Mr. Hull, and their coadjutors, has been published. Geological maps, giving proprietors useful information with respect to the minerals likely to be found on their domains, have been printed and sold. For some twenty years the nation has employed a highly paid band of geologists in discovering the mineral wealth of the kingdom, and in the results of their labours the State has not directly participated. The owner of the fee-simple has taken everything. Translated into the language which we have employed in the previous chapters, the substance of all that has been said with reference to mines is, that landowners draw purely 'economical rent,' and they draw it from natural agencies of which they are making daily new appropriations. The condition of affairs with respect to the sites of cities has the excuse of being of old standing ; that excuse is absent in the case of mines; it is a wrong system daily receiving fresh applications.

To complete the story, let me add that most mines have been the subject of a remarkable and

little-noted exemption with respect to rating—an
exemption worth to their proprietors hundreds of
thousands.   The Act of Elizabeth, which is the
basis of our rating system, mentions among the
rateable species of property coal mines and none
else.   So, on the principle *expressio unius exclusio
alterius*, it was held that iron and other mines
were exempted.   What was the reason of this
apparently unaccountable difference in treatment
is not known ; but it may be, as Baron Martin
suggested, that the framers of the Act deemed mines
other than coal were of the nature of manufactories
carried on by means of ore.[1]   At any rate, the
House of Lords felt itself compelled to declare that
all mines save coal mines are exempted from rating
for the relief of the poor.   Indeed, an attempt was
lately made, though unsuccessfully, to claim exemption for the buildings, workshops, and machinery
attached to ironworks, as being the accessories of
unrateable property.[2]

It may be interesting to enquire what would be

---

[1] *Morgan* v. *Crashaw,* V. L. R. A. C. 304.

[2] *Guest* v. *Dean,* VII. L. R. Q.B. 331.

the gain, supposing that the State acquired 'the economical rent of mines.' It is a problem fraught with difficulties, owing to ignorance of the future rate of development of the coal and iron industries of this and other countries. The Northern Alleghany coalfields alone, and the iron deposits of North America, chiefly confined to Pennsylvania, are capable of yielding limitless stores, and we do not know when they may be extensively worked. But, if no important industrial change take place, and if England still continue to supply the world with metals, there cannot fail to come a time when the assumption by the State of the right to the minerals, subject to existing interests, would prove a step of great profit. In the first place, there is reason to believe that no little gain would be acquired at once and without any grant of compensation. To geologists and miners, it is a familiar fact that the old ideas touching the common situation of minerals are changing rapidly. Often they are found where our ancestors held that they could not exist. The history of Cornish mining abundantly illustrates this truth ; and I shall mention one in-

stance. It was an old adage that 'tin never made
in depth.' It was to be got, according to the miner,
in the junction of the granite and 'killas,' near the
surface. Watt, Trevethick, and the use of gun-
powder changed the miner's ideas on this point;
and, with improved modes of working, this notion
is now exploded.[1] Look next at the subversion of
the customary ideas with respect to the site of coal.
They, too, are being shaken by a thousand investi-
gators. I have mentioned the novel contention for
which Mr. Prestwich elaborately argues in an appendix to the report of the Coal Commission ; and
there have of late been borings which reveal the
existence of coal in the South of England to an
extent never before dreamt of. Under Dorsetshire
there seems to lie workable coal. Excavations at
Sandwell Park, near Birmingham, seem to indicate
the unity of the South Staffordshire, Warwickshire,
and Shropshire fields ; and shafts sunk on the Duke
of Newcastle's estate at the Shire Oaks in Nottinghamshire, and on the Earl of Granville's estate at

---

[1] 'It is observed that tin rarely continues worth working beyond fifty fathoms deep.'—Polwhele's *Cornwall*, vol. iv. p. 133.

Lilleshall in Shropshire, seem to show that immediately under the Permian formation may be got coals at the present remunerative depth. Even the axiom that coal and lignite worth using are confined to the newer Palæozoic period may yet be shaken.[1]

So far the yet undiscovered minerals or *bona vacantia*, and the probability that they would prove valuable to the State. In the case of deposits actually worked there seems, in view of the recent increase in the prices of coal and iron, to be pre-eminent justification for the application of Mr. Mill's proposal for the absorption of ' the unearned increase.' If it were said that all future rises in the rent of mines should become the property of the community, the injustice which would be done is not very apparent; if the change were fixed to take place ten or twenty years hence, it would be non-existent.

Few would deny that any immunities with respect to rating ought to be removed; and it may be submitted that more might be done. Though it is impossible to determine what should be the limit of the time necessary for the owners of mines to

[1] Ansted's *Geology*, vol. ii. p. 328.

recoup themselves, we may be sure that thirty or
forty years would be sufficient; assuredly, if they
were permitted to extract, by means of royalties
and other emoluments, all which they could obtain
during that period, their just cause of complaint
would be small were Parliament to appropriate the
reversion. Yet, rather than do aught that savoured
of injustice, it might be expedient to pay now the
reversionary value, and allow all life interests to
run out. Such a step might prove safe and just to
both vendor and purchaser.

Rapid as has been the advance in the value of
agricultural and urban land, still more surprising
has been the increase in the value of mineral
property. While the rateable value of mines
(exclusive of ironworks, quarries, and salt and
alum works) increased 25 per cent. between 1862
and 1870, the rateable value of land increased only
6 per cent. Of ironworks the annual value has
increased still more rapidly; in 1862, the annual
produce was 1,079,589*l.*, and in 1870 it was
2,018,564*l.* In other words, there was an advance of
50 per cent. In the raising of coals there is a like

advance; the value of the coals raised in 1857 amounted to 16,348,676*l.*; and in 1870 it had swollen to 27,607,798*l.* It may, therefore, be with confidence predicted that no small amount of revenue could be derived from this source.

CHAPTER VII.

COMMONS AND WASTE LANDS.

THERE is a rich leaven of antiquity in all that pertains to the common lands of England; and he who would understand their present position must know their past. Acquaintance with history is highly useful for the comprehension of any portion of our land tenure, for we dwell in a building constructed by many hands—one on which we may trace the marks of the tools of Celt and Saxon and Norman, primitive communism and feudalism; and there is a certain mystery of antiquity about our customary holdings. Such knowledge is absolutely essential to one who would know how the law relating to commons came to be what it is.

The text books do not always give their true history, and the phraseology of English law is apt to conceal it. Under the misleading name of ' custom ' the remains of ancient law are buried; by the copious supposition of fictitious deeds of grants, the preserved fragments of earlier systems are explained away; and in the Common Law of England relative to this subject are huddled together ideas of property discordant and of different origin. It is only of late that our judges begin to cast doubts on the customary professional explanations of such peculiarities of English law as copyholds and rights of common appendant and appurtenant.[1] Only gradually is it dawning upon legal writers and practitioners how feudalism failed to submerge earlier forms of property, and how lusty shoots of institutions older than the Conquest have survived and flourished in England. Truth on such points is not of purely antiquarian interest. From this brief and imperfect sketch of the inclosure or 'approvement' of commons, it will appear what substantial wrong has been done in obedience to false history and black-letter fictions. The English landowner coveted the wastes attached to his manor. The story of his

[1] See Lord Hatherley's judgment in *Warrick* v. *Queen's College.* VI. L.R. C.A. 716.

grasping efforts to acquire them forms the burden
of this chapter. But it was necessary or expedient
to drape spoliation in the robes of legality ; and this
service to covetousness, perhaps natural, the English
lawyers rendered, telling the lord of the manor that
he did but resume his own, speaking to him of grants
which were never made, and affirming that the freehold of the coveted waste was originally in him. Had
the true history of English commons been known,
they would have been divided very differently.

What were the oldest forms of property in
Britain there is little evidence. Cæsar says that the
majority of those who lived in the interior did not
sow corn. Probably the land, so far as it was
cultivated at all, was parcelled out in much the
same way in which we find it among various
Celtic tribes. We therefore turn to them. In Ireland and the Highlands of Scotland there existed,
even in historical times, a form of communism.
The Highland clan or sept owned the strath or glen
wherein it dwelt. No man held his land in perpetuity, to be disposed of as he might dictate.
When a clansman died, his allotment might be

divided. The chief was only the officer of the clan; his post was not necessarily hereditary; and it is matter of history that one sept, the Macdonalds of Clanranald, actually exiled their chieftain and slew him in battle. The Highlander could not be taught the justice of the feudal idea of property, which connected every acre with some lord. It long remained to the Celt ' hateful and scarcely comprehensible.' Not regarding the ownership of their native glen as lodged in the chief alone, the clansmen could not be persuaded that his treason justly involved the forfeiture of land which was theirs as much as his. So when the Government seized the estates of the chiefs who had taken an active part in the rebellion of 1745, the clansmen looked upon the newcomers as intruders, and we know that purchasers of the confiscated estates were with difficulty found.[1] A dweller in Lochaber is rudely evicted from his dwelling by a Government agent; by-and-by, while the instrument of the law, a Captain Munro of Culcairn, rides through the glen at the head of an armed

---

[1] See Notes to *Waverley.*

P

party, he is shot by some vindicator of tenant right.[1]
Another agent of the Government, Campbell of
Glenure, gives mortal offence by turning out certain
old tenants, and he is forthwith shot also.   Though
the lands of the rebel chieftains were forfeited, the
clansmen, who knew and respected a tenure outside
the law, gave them unforced allegiance ; and Lochiel
and Ardsheal, living in banishment in France, for
years received their rents from retainers who like-
wise paid the same dues to the Crown.

   There was, indeed, a tradition preserved by
Lord Kames that Malcolm Canmore had introduced
feudalism into Scotland, and had given in feudal
grants the whole soil, with the exception of the
Mutehill of Scoon.   But what matter to the clansman
that then or in the times of David I., to whom more
credible history pointed as the true author of Scotch
feudalism, there had been imported the alien feudal
system, with all its apparatus and jargon of *a me*
and *de me*?[2]   What mattered a charter issued by

---

[1] Stewart's *Highlands*, vol. i. appendix iv.
[2] 'The very oldest writ in the shape of a charter connected
with Scotland is that of Duncan, the son of Malcolm Canmore,

the *Rex Scottorum?* The clansman was no con-
senting party, and he could not be reconciled to
changes which made him a mere tenant at will.
The circumstance that a notary public had tra-
velled from Edinburgh to a remote glen, and there,
perhaps in the middle of a moor, with the aid
of two clerks and the postboy, had given 'infeft-
ment' of the surrounding country, did not satisfy
the Highlander that his rights were extinguished.[1]
For centuries he persisted in preferring the sept
chiefs to those whom feudalism had given him.
The Duke of Gordon, nominally lord of a large
tract of country, could not bring into the field so
many swords as his feudatory, Macdonald of Clanranald, who, though described in the account of the
clans compiled by order of President Forbes as
a mere 'tacksman,' commanded a following of 200
men-at-arms. In the rebellion of 1745, nothing is
more surprising than the large number of men
whom petty landowners or mere subvassals could

the date of which is about 1094. With David I. really begins
our body of Scotch charters.'—Innes's *Lectures on Scotch
Legal Antiquities*, p. 29.

[1] More's *Lectures on the Law of Scotland*, vol. i. p. 480.

equip. And when it ceased to be the interest of
the Highland chiefs to maintain a large body of retainers, and when they began to imitate the ruthless
evictions which had been employed in England in the
reigns of Henry VII., Henry VIII., and Edward VI.,
the clansmen again resented, as cruel quibbles, the
legal machinery which Bailie Macwheebles brought
out in order to strip them of their customary rights.
The evictions of Sutherlandshire, and the rise in
rents which took place all over the Highlands after
the general introduction of sheep farming, were
regarded as usurpations.

In Orkney and Shetland we meet with the udal
tenure, which arose when these islands were subject
to the Crown of Denmark. Lands originally paid,
it is said, a tax or tribute called *skat*; and, as they
were cultivated and enclosed, they were released
from this tribute and became udal or allodial, that
is, held of no superior, and in virtue of no charter
from the Crown or anyone claiming under it.[1]

Such were the early systems of land tenure
scattered over Scotland—systems accompanied,

[1] More's *Lectures*, vol. i. p. 466. Bell's *Commentaries*.

perhaps necessarily, by rude husbandry. There was no rotation of crops; the turf peeled off some neighbouring land, and placed on what the clansman wished to improve, formed what was, not inappropriately, termed 'a lazybed;' and he tilled his little farm, if he tilled it at all, on the 'infield' and 'outfield' system, that is, he cultivated the land nearest his hut badly, and the portion more remote a little worse.

For centuries after the nominal conquest of Ireland, the English Common Law did not travel beyond the Pale, which comprehended six conquered counties. Until the reign of James I., the Brehon Law ruled the greater part of that country. The Statute of Kilkenny had indeed declared the Brehon Law to be a 'lewd custom;' but only in the reign of James I. was it conclusively decided that the very prevalent custom of tanistry was illegal.[1] In the words of Sir John Davies, it was held to be unreasonable, and therefore illegal, because a commonwealth cannot exist without a certain ownership of land

[1] The case of tanistry. *Murragh Mac Bryan* v. *Cahir O'Callaghan.* Davies' *Reports in the King's Bench, Ireland,* p. 78.

'and because, if men know not certainly for what person they travail and defraud their souls of pleasure, as Solomon saith, they will never improve their land to the best use, nor build houses of any value, nor give civil education to their children ; but, having respect to their present time only, they will be utterly careless of posterity.'

Perhaps the clearest exposition of the ancient Irish land system is to be found in the resolutions of the judges touching ' the Irish custom of gavelkind.' All possessions before the introduction of the Common Law of England, they say, ' ran always either in course of tanistry or in course of gavelkind.' Every seignory or chiefry, with the land which passed with it, went without partition to the tanist or heir apparent, who came in by election or the strong hand, and not by descent. At the death of a clansman, the whole of the estates of the sept might be thrown into hotch-potch, and a new partition was made by the chief ; ' in which partition he did not assign to the son of him who died the portion which his father had, but he allotted to each of the sept, according to his seniority, the better or greater

portion.'[1] In other words, succession was determined by the custom of tanistry—the land passed to
the oldest and worthiest of the family, *seniori et
dignissimo viro ejusdem sanguinis et cognominis.*
The Brehon Laws reveal many phases of early Irish
land tenure. In the ' saer ' stock and ' daer ' stock
tenures, we find the equivalents of the metayer
tenure in common use abroad, and of the steel-
bow tenancy to be met with in Scotland, that is, a
tenure according to which the chief furnishes his
vassal with cattle. ' What are the returns of each
' sed,' or due amount of stock supplies from great to
small, in ' saer' stock tenure? ' The answer of the
' Senchus Mor ' is : ' In three years the chief is entitled to a " sed " in addition to that already given.'[2]
In ' daer' stock tenancy, which was optional, the
tenant paid so much as ' honour price ' to the chief,
and so much in proportion to the stock supplied.
' The chief's claim for rent was contingent on his
supplying stock to the occupiers of his land.'[3]

[1] Resolution of the judges touching the Irish custom of
Gavelkind. Davies' *Report*, p. 134.

[2] *Ancient Laws of Ireland*, vol. ii.

[3] *Ibid.* p. xlviii.

Accustomed to regard the land as more or less the property of the sept, the Irish septman, like his brother Celt in Scotland, did not relish the English ideas which made him a mere tenant of a superior lord. His chief's crimes he could not regard as annulling his claims; and the O'Mores and the O'Connors took up arms against those who would deprive them of their lands on account of the political offences of their chieftains. Though much was done to efface this feeling—though in his time Lord Clare could say with truth to the Irish landowners, 'Confiscation is your common title'—though we are told that 11,697,629 acres were confiscated between the reign of James I. and the revolution of 1688—the feeling still lingers. Centuries of English rule have not obliterated it. The offshoots of 'the lewd customs' may survive the system that came to destroy them.

I ought here to mention a peculiar form of tenure—runrig or rundale—to be found alike in England, Scotland, and Ireland. Sometimes the land was split up into thin compartments or strips,

each of which belonged to a different owner.
Even so late as the end of last century the landowners of Donegal were busy uprooting a system
manifestly incompatible with good husbandry. One
witness before the Devon Commission, Lord George
Hill, stated that he knew a person who held his land in
forty-two different patches, and who ' at last gave it
up in despair of finding it.' The system existed all
over Scotland ; and as it split the land into strips too
narrow for ploughing, and was generally contrary
to good husbandry, in 1695 the Scotch Parliament
passed an Act for the division in severalty of land
held in runrig.[1] The reports of decisions in the Court
of Session during the last century and the beginning
of the present century are full of actions for the
division of land lying in runrig or runridge.[2] The
same custom we meet with in England, the soil of
which was frequently divided into minute panes or
compartments. The parish of Chinnor in Oxford,
for example, was split up into some two thousand

[1] *Erskine*, book iii. tit. iii. p. 59.
[2] *Douglas* v. *Forrest*, January 21, 1777.

patches, each of the average size of three roods, twenty-three perches.[1]

In the fifth and subsequent centuries there came to England Angles, Saxons, and Jutes, bringing with them their institutions and customs.[2]   Describing the Germans of his time, Cæsar distinctly states that they did not know fixed property in land : each year there was a redistribution of it among the sept. In his *Germania*, Tacitus, describing the same people two centuries later, mentions that the soil was at intervals—perhaps no longer annually—divided, a device probably employed to assure equality of value in portions.   To England, then, came those Jutes, Saxons, and Angles, and settling there, they formed, we are told, the *pagus* or mark.   Among the chief and his followers, or comrades, were parcelled out portions of the soil, to be held in absolute ownership, and known as the edel or allodial land.   On the out-

[1] Mr. Blamire's evidence before the Committee on Commons' Inclosure.

[2] Proofs of the unity of those early forms of property and laws are accumulating.   For example, it is clear that the custom of fosterage, a singular form of adoption, once supposed to be peculiar to Ireland, existed in England and Wales. See *Ancient Laws of Ireland*, vol. ii. No. xlvi.

skirts of the mark lay the waste, belonging to the community and undivided. This, it is surmised, was the origin of the 'folcland' or *ager publicus*. According to Kemble, it was the result of the union of two or more wastes or marclands. Over this folcland, or people's land, no man had more than possessory rights. He could not freely devise his interest. It did not descend to his heirs. It was subject to the burthen of the *trinoda necessitas*, from which, indeed, no land was free, that is to say, the landowner must be ready to do military service, and to repair the king's highways and his castles. We are told that there went on a process which steadily reduced the size of the folcland. With the consent of the Witan or popular Assembly, the king could make grants out of the common domain; and these grants, being booked or publicly entered, became known as bocland, and were placed in the same position as edel or allodial land. Such land bore the burthen of the *trinoda necessitas*, but it was subject to no other dues. Then came a change, the steps of which are obscure. The king's power increases; the Witan loses its influence; the king's *comitatus* or personal following, grows in importance; the ceorl's lot deteriorates; and the magnitude of the *Comitatus* almost places the king in the position of a monarch of feudal times. By-and-by each man is bound to attach himself to some lord; and long before feudalism exists by name, and before the *Consuetudines Feudorum* are written, we witness feudalism full blown, if its essence be, as Wright, for example, alleges, the rendering of fealty. Economical and political movements are wont to travel in parallel lines, and the same causes which were destroying the old democratic forms of Government were effacing the democratic character of property. The antiquated notion, set forth by Madox and Reeve for example, that William, by a single *statuimus* created feudalism, seems unfounded; and though it may not be quite true, as Sir Francis Palgrave roundly affirms, that ' there is the strongest evidence ' that the Conquest did not make any difference in the tenure of land, it seems certain that the common theory with respect to two features in particular, copyholds and commons, is erroneous.

If history speaks of revolutions and cataclysms

rather than of growth, it is because history is imperfect. Fuller knowledge reveals intermediate steps; and the more one knows of the Conquest the more one is assured that old English institutions survived and triumphed over the conquerors. Such seems the truth with respect to the commons of England.

If we try to picture from the accounts of lawyers the state of England after the Conquest, we shall conceive England parcelled into manors, over each of which presides some lord. From the king flowed all rights of property; to him the lords owed allegiance and service. To inferior tenants they make grants or subfeus, on condition of receiving certain dues. Perhaps the vassal was bound to serve his lord in war. If the tenure was of a base kind, he might be bound to labour so many days in his lord's fields. The Pusey estates were held on condition that the owner should always keep a certain horn. Some towns possessed of land were required to furnish one day's entertainment for the king. Domesday Book enables one to eke out the picture. We read of the tenant *in capite*, or great lords who held of the king; the thanes or vavasours, nobles whose exact status is uncertain; *aloarii*, whose lands were allodial and subject only to a land tax; *liberi homines*, or freemen of all conditions, some of them hangers on of a great lord, others subject to none but the king; sochemanni, who held their land in *soc* or franchise of some lord; and a great mass of serfs and slaves.

There is much evidence that there was not a complete dislocation of society. The country still lived very much its old life, under new masters. The bulk of the people still belonged to agricultural communities, more or less perfect. Many, perhaps most, of the Saxon proprietors retained their lands, and on the same terms as those to which they were subject under the Confessor. The manors may have been but the continuation of the old marks, which had ceased to be democratic. There were still the old local courts, somewhat changed indeed, but substantially the same as those of ante-Norman times. There was the Court Baron, to which came the lord of the manor and the freemen. There was also the Court Customary, to which the copyholders repaired with their peculiar grievances. In these

Courts were determined all matters concerning the land of the manor. In these and other institutions traces or fragments of the old village community still existed; and 'Domesday Book' abounds with proofs that the 'vill' or township had its rights as well as the landlord. There is mention of common belonging 'to all men,' and 'pasture for the cattle of the village' is a frequent entry.[1]

Over England are still scattered remains of the old *régime*, which the Conquest modified but did not destroy—remains of a time when, to quote Marshall, 'each parish or township was considered one common farm, though the tenantry were numerous.' In his work on the agriculture of Yorkshire, he describes the old system as existing almost perfect in the vale of Pickering. Round the village lay the common farmstead or homestead; next were the arable fields allotted to winter and summer crops and fallow; then came the meadow grounds, or 'ings;' and beyond lay the commonable lands and commons, which were sometimes locally spoken of as 'the known lands' and 'half-year

[1] Sir Henry Ellis' *Introduction to Domesday*, vol. i. pp. 103, 171.

lands,' that is, tracts open at all seasons, or after Lammas. In certain districts there were practices similar to rundale or runrig. What Tacitus wrote of their fathers—*arva per annos mutant*—was true of many Englishmen of recent times; and the land so apportioned was known as 'dale' or 'lot meadow.' Sometimes the best lot fell to the most successful wrestler. In 'the sheep heaves' of the North of England, and the 'cattle gates,' familiar to every Yorkshireman, and not unknown to lawyers as the subject of no small litigation, there are the remains of the same *régime*.

In Domesday Book there are many allusions to waste lands. At the date of its compilation the country was sparsely peopled; and in every manor there must have been much of the soil unculti- vated and open. The commons may have been part of the unabsorbed folcland or the 'mearc- land,' or waste around the old mark.[1] It is pro- bable that as the power of the king rose, and that of the Witan waned, most of the folcland was swallowed up by the former, and became known

---

[1] Allen *On the Royal Prerogative*, p. 152.

as Crown land.[1] Some portions not so dealt with, as being too poor, may have been the origin of commons. They may, indeed, have been included in the grants made to the lords by kings; but the rights of common existed before the lord existed. Certainly there is no proof that what is now common was ever allodial or bocland, or that rights of common were ever, as a matter of fact, granted by the lord. The truth seems to be that the lord of the manor's right was more of an usurpation than the so-called customs in favour of his tenant. No doubt, the lord was more released from the control of the community than was the ealdorman. But there were laws binding on the former also. It does not appear, the dictum of Lord Coke notwith-

---

[1] The origin of the commons in Scotland is usually alleged to be much the same as in England. 'Commonty,' says Professor Bell, 'arose at first from grants made by feudal lords and proprietors to their feuors and tenants of rights to pasture their cattle on the grazing ground or waste of the barony. Sometimes, also, cottages were suffered, by vicinage and custom, to establish a right of common over those and waste pasture lands. Neighbouring towns, too, permitted reciprocal encroachments on their pasture ground, and so established commonty of pasture by mutual agreement or forbearance.' —Bell's *Commentaries*, vol. ii. p. 800.

standing, that the lord of the manor could 'approve' or enclose without the consent of his tenants before the Statute of Merton. The operative words of that statute, and those of its supplement the Statute of Westminster,[1] are inconsistent with the contrary notion, though sanctioned by such high authority as Coke and Justice Buller.

There is proof in the earliest law books and statutes of the importance of commons and waste lands. In Glanville, one of the earliest writers on English law, we find specimens of writs to the sheriffs to provide for cases of usurpation.[2] Bracton, who wrote on the customs and laws of England in the reign of Henry III., discusses the subject of commons at much length. He states that rights of commons were acquired by grant, sale, long use, *ex scientia, negligentia, et patientia dominorum*, and that they might be so lost. He speaks of the remedies open to one who was deprived of such rights. The sufferer was to go to the person who looks after such rights to obtain assize or a writ of enquiry, for the purpose of recovery. It was the duty of the

[1] 20 Henry III. c. 4, and 13 Edward I. c. 46.
[2] *Glanville*, p. 275. Beame's translation.

vicecomes, or sheriff, to examine such complaints without delay. A jury was to be empanelled, and, in the presence of the parties, it was bound to inquire into the alleged grievances, and to certify to the justices the results of the examination. Bracton did little more than apply to commons the doctrines of the Roman law relative to servitudes.[1] It was left to other lawyers to draw the distinction between easements and *profits à prendre*, or mere rights over the soil and profits therefrom, which Bracton had lumped together. By-and-by there was also elaborated the distinction between common appendant and common appurtenant, or rights of common possessed by the tenant of a manor as an incident to his land and rights conferred by special grant.[2] A long series of cases, from *Gateward's* case to our own time, has built up the present complicated law of common rights.

[1] *Dunraven* v. *Llewelyn*, 15 Q.B. 791.

[2] Güterbock, who has inquired into the relations of Bracton's work to the Civil Law, observes that its influence on his teaching is not very perceptible with respect to commons. Two maxims, however, Bracton plainly owes to the civil law—first, that the rights of common could exist only in connection with land, and that they must exist over another man's land.

Even in Bracton's time the work of enclosing had begun ; and he speaks of many lords not being able to make good use of their manors by reason of the claims of commoners. So it was provided that were it shown that the tenants had been left sufficient pasture, with free egress and ingress, then ' let them be content therewith,' and let their lords be free to enjoy the improvements which they have effected in their lands, wastes, and pastures. It was the Statute of Merton which gave, or, as some say, confirmed this power.[1] In the Year Books we find many instances of attempts to 'approve;' for example, in one of the Year Books of Edward I. there is chronicled an attempt to enclose, under the Statute of Merton, contrary to the terms of a reservation of common of pasture in a feoffment.[2] In the same Year Book we note another attempt again made under the Statute of Merton to approve contrary to the terms of a grant.[3] In the Year Book for 1304, there is mention of a writ of admeasurement against

[1] 20 Henry III. c. 4., supplemented by the Statute of Westminster, 13 Edward I. c. 46.

[2] Year Books of Edward I., for years 30–31 (Harwood's edition), p. 353.   [3] Ibid. p. 328.

certain lords of the ' vill ' of C., for surcharging the
common pasture with more beasts than they were
entitled to in proportion to their freeholds; and
Bereford, J., lays it down that if the lord ' surcharge
so that the tenant cannot have a sufficient pasture, I
say he is a disseisor.'

The *Extenta Manerii*, a statute said to have
been passed in the fourth year of the reign of
Edward I., directs inquiries to be made as to the
extent of the lord's right of pasture outside his manor
and of the amount of land which he was at liberty
to improve. For many years the statute book received few new enactments on the subject. Yet,
in the reign of Edward IV., the lord of the manor
obtained one clear victory. It was decided that
the inhabitants of a town, a fluctuating uncertain
number, could not have common of pasture.[1] For
a time, labour rather than land was in demand;
and there were passed many laws, such as the
Statute of Labourers, which complain of the exces-
sive wages of husbandry and of the efforts of the
bondmen to break away from their yoke.[2] In the

[1] 6 Rep. 59. [2] See Eden's *State of Poor*, vol. i. p. 36.

reign of Edward VI., Parliament solemnly resanc-
tioned the Statute of Merton. Certainly, the work
of enclosure did not stand still. John Rous, who
writes in the end of the fifteenth century, is fierce
in his denunciations of the enclosers of his time,
declaring that they insulted God and man by 'their
preference of irrational beasts to rational men.'[1]
Thomas More, writing later, speaks of the sheep
as becoming so voracious that 'they devour men,
fields, and houses, and desolate and depopulate
towns.' Bernard Gilpin treats as worse than Ahab
those who pluck away the pastures of the com-
monalty and 'who sell the poor for a pair of
shoes.' True, the statutes of Henry III. and
Edward I., under which enclosures took place,
declared that the tenants were to be left sufficient
pasture. But, as Latimer pointedly asked, 'Who
should be the judge to limit what was sufficient for
them?' If the statutes of Henry III. and Edward I.,
argued Latimer, allowed the landlords to take
away so much pasture from the tenants, the lords
would be sure to leave no more than was barely

---

[1] Cited in Brodie's *Constitutional History*.

sufficient; 'and if the tenants had any more taken from them since that time, then they had not now sufficient.'[1]

In the reigns of Henry VII. and Henry VIII. were passed numerous laws, the object of which was to prevent land being turned into pasturage. In the time of the latter alone were passed no fewer than four Acts, levelled against 'pulling doune and destruction of tounes wythin thys realme and laying to pasture landes which customably have been manured and occupied wyth tyllage and husbandry.' Still the work of enclosure went on. These Acts of Parliament and the denunciation of Latimer could not prevent the spoliation of the poor. In 1548 Cornwall was in a state of revolt, chiefly by reason of this cause of vexation. So the Lord Protector issued a proclamation against the enclosing of arable lands and turning them into pasture, a policy which, he said, had brought the land to 'a marvellous desolation.' He also appointed a royal commission of inquiry. As was pointed out by John Hales, one of the Commissioners, in his charge, the inquiry

[1] Last sermon preached before King Edward VI.

was designed to lead to the enforcement of the
Acts passed in the preceding reigns.   It did not
bear much fruit.   The Chronicles of Strype for the
next year are full of the records of fresh riots.
Of course, the enclosures complained of did not
as a rule relate to commons.   But they frequently
related to Lammas lands subject to rights of common.

We need not follow minutely the later history
of the enclosures of commons.   It is enough to say
that in every county history will be read the records
of the strife.   Each village green has created
Hampdens, who withstood the little tyrants or Ahabs
of the fields.   One could name commons which
have been saved to the poor by bravery and adroit-
ness which, on a larger platform, would have been
memorable in history.   Let us narrate only one
instance ; but let us think of it as typical of many.
Berkhampstead Common or Frith was part of the
honour of Berkhampstead, which was granted to
the Prince of Wales in the reign of Edward III.   It
at one time included 1,270 acres.   In 1618 the
Prince of Wales of that time appropriated 300
acres, and added them to his park.   This step was

taken with the consent of the tenants; and in 1639 400 more acres were enclosed and leased. But this new encroachment the people would not brook, and one William Edlyn, of North Church, figures dimly in law reports as a sort of stalwart Hampden of his time. He threw down the new fences. The Commissioners of the Revenues of the Prince of Wales petitioned Parliament, and complained of the rudeness of Edlyn. The House of Lords ordered Edlyn not to repeat the offence, and said that the Prince should enjoy the enclosed lands during that Parliament. In 1651 the honour and manor were sold to Godfrey Ellis and Griffontius Philips; and Ellis offered 400 acres for sale. The indefatigable Edlyn in 1653 presented a petition to certain Commissioners ' for the removing of obstructions in the sale of the honours of the late King and Queen and Prince,' and prayed that Ellis should be compelled to make out the State's title. Ellis failed to give security for costs of inquiry, and the result was that all fresh enclosures were stopped. And so John Edlyn passes out of sight. But we owe him much. He kept the common intact until 1866, when Earl

Brownlow again attempted to enclose it, and was foiled by Mr. Augustus Smith.[1]

The machinery of the Acts of Merton and Westminster moved too slowly for the landowners, and particularly because it did not enable them to enclose against the wishes of copyholders. It was, therefore, customary to resort to private Acts of Parliament. In the reigns of the Georges the work of enclosure was carried on with zeal and even fury. Lovers of rural beauty, and pitiful souls such as Goldsmith, deplored the ravages made in the name of agriculture and improvement.

> Those fenceless fields the sons of wealth divide,
> And even the bareworn common is denied.

On the other hand, men who looked to material results, asked why they should send 7,000,000*l.* abroad in three years in order to purchase corn, while so much of the soil of England was wasted or misapplied. What excuse, it was asked, could be given for the maintenance of commonable lands? And how could winter wheat be sown if there was a

[1] 9 L.R. Equity 241.

flockmaster who at a certain season was entitled to
depasture his sheep over a whole parish? One
writer declared that the value of the whole produce
of common land did not amount to more than four
shillings an acre.[1] Perhaps to Arthur Young more
than any other is due this rage for enclosing. In
and out of season he preached it. ' The greatest
disgrace to a kingdom so truly flourishing is the
existence of so much waste land ; ' and he pledged
himself to pay off the National Debt in a few years
by running the plough through the idle acres of
the North of England. He groaned in spirit over
the moorland farms of Northumberland, yielding a
slovenly crop for a year or two, and then suffered
to fall into grass. ' What a noble source of riches
and population ! '[2] he exclaims, as he looks at the
broad moors stretching between Alnwick and Roth-
bury. ' At a slight expense every acre might be
made worth 8s. to 10s.' Marshall, an agricultural
writer of the end of last century and the beginning

---

[1] Middleton's *Survey of Middlesex*. Quoted in Southey's
Doctor, vol. i. p. 197.

[2] *Six Months' Tour through the North of England*, vol iii.
p. 86.

of this, dwelt much on the pernicious effect of commons and commonable lands; Lammas land he computes to be worth only one half of similar land when enclosed.

The portion of the poor was all the while being silently absorbed. There were few to befriend him in the jostle of landowners and an unreformed Parliament; and oftentimes the cotter had only a confused idea that something was going on in that remote and inconceivable centre of things, London, before he learned that he might no more drive afield his geese and cows. These things were done in corners; they did not come before the eye of the world; and in the private Acts passed before 1800, there was small attention paid to the wants of the poor. Unrepresented and undefended, their rights were swept away. The work of destruction was facilitated not a little by the general Act passed at the instance of Sir George Sinclair, which consolidated certain provisions usually inserted in all enclosure Acts; and, by its aid, in the space of forty-five years there were passed 2,000 private enclosure bills. Yet the work did not go on fast enough to satisfy landowners. The expense of procuring a private bill was very large, and it might amount to a thousand pounds. In fairness let us add that scandalous instances of waste were to be met with in the more thickly peopled counties; in Lancashire alone there were 200,000 acres of uncultivated land. Commonable land still abounded. Accordingly there was passed the 6 and 7 Will. IV. c. 115, facilitating enclosures; and in 1845 there was enacted the General Enclosure Act, which is the chief instrument of recent enclosures.[1] It did not become law without opposition. Men so dissimilar as Mr. Joseph Hume and Colonel Sibthorp agreed in denouncing it as a landlord's bill. Yet it triumphed over them. It became law in a form which Parliament has since repented of. Commissioners were to be appointed to carry out the Act. They were empowered to see to the enclosure of commons, and 'gates and stinted pasture;' but 'no waste land of any manor on which the tenants of such manor have rights of common, nor any land whatsoever subject to rights of common which may be exercised

---

[1] 8 & 9 Vic. c. 118.

at all times of every year, for cattle levant or couchant upon other land, or to any rights of common which may be exercised at all times of every year, and which shall not be limited by number of stints, shall be enclosed under this Act, without the previous authority of Parliament in each particular case.' A similar limitation was imposed upon enclosures within fifteen miles of London, and within smaller distances from other large cities. The interests of commoners, if claimed in respect of land, were to be valued according to its rateable value ; if in respect of rights of common in gross rated to the relief of the poor, and not ' defined by numbers and stint,' the interests were to be valued as the Commissioners might determine. This Act was the turning point in legislation. Since the passing of it Parliament has set its face in the opposite direction.

I come now to nearly the last of the enactments on the subject, and of the few it will be unnecessary to mention all. In 1866 there was passed an enactment which made it permissible to enclose certain portions of the Forest of Dean, which the General Enclosure Act of 1845 had specially exempted.

Subsequently there was passed the Metropolitan Commons Act,[1] which declared that 'after the passing of this Act the Commissioners shall not entertain an application for the enclosure of a Metropolitan Common, or any part thereof,' and which provided schemes 'for the establishment of local management.' This Act allowed the Metropolitan Board of Works to compensate those who were damaged or destroyed by any such scheme; and under the powers of this Act it has purchased Hampstead Heath. Subsequently, in 1869, the Act was extended to all land subject to the General Enclosure Act of 1845.

Let us now glance at the mode in which the commons or commonties of Scotland have been enclosed or divided for nearly two centuries. In that country there has been since 1695 ample machinery for their enclosure. An Act of that year, singularly influential in its effect on Scotch agriculture and life, declares that 'all commonties, except the commonties belonging to the king and royal boroughs in burgage, may be divided at the

---

[1] 29 & 30 Vic. c. 122, amended by 32 & 33 Vic. c. 107.

instance of any having interest, by summons raised against all persons concerned before the Lords of Session.' It was wisely provided in this Act that it should not affect the commonties belonging to royal boroughs. But this precaution was made somewhat worthless by two decisions of the Court of Session, which declared that when the commonty had not been conveyed to a corporation on behalf of the inhabitants, but merely to the burgesses, a division might take place.[1] On the whole, the results of the Act have been by no means entirely satisfactory. There is every reason to believe that the poor have frequently been greatly despoiled by _the Act of 1695. Lawyers used the doctrines of feudalism to the detriment of commoners. ' They pointed,' says Professor Innes, ' to his (the baron's) charter, with its clause of parts and pertinents, with its general clause of mosses and moors—clauses taken from the style book, not with any reference to the territory conveyed in that charter; and, although the charter was hundreds of years old, and the lord had never

---

[1] *White* v. *Calder*, February 13, 1812, and *Henderson* v. *Malcolm*, June 29, 1815.

possessed any of the common, when it came to be divided, the lord got the whole that was allocated to his estate, and the poor cotter none.'¹ No allotment is made on behalf of those who are not proprietors, or who do not possess the right to cut turf or other servitudes over the commonty; and for a time it was customary for the proprietor of the *solum* to receive a *præcipuum* or bonus slice over and above the shares allotted to those whose rights were mere servitudes or easements. 'The present writer recollects listening to a Scotch farmer pouring forth his treasured wrath at the spoliation of what he held to be his birthright. Bleak was the hill to which he pointed with indignation, and little to be prized, thought the on-looker, were the saffron-coloured swamps which hung on the hill flanks, or the thin, rugged, seamy soil through which the rocks protruded. But his father's cattle had fed there, and he perhaps had cut turf in the few green dells, and it had in the past been "our hill," and it was a loss to him not measured by guineas to be obliged to look over a wire fence or

¹ Innes' *Scotch Legal Antiquities*, p. 155.

a whinstone dyke at what had once been virtually his.' [1]

The process of division is strictly litigious. The person who desires a division proceeds to make the parties interested defendants to a friendly suit. In the 'condescendence' which accompanies the summons, he sets out his grounds for believing that the common in question is a fit subject for division. The other parties then lodge statements of the nature and extent of their claims and their pleas in law. The record having been closed, and the applicant's or pursuer's title having been sustained, the Lord Ordinary will direct a surveyor to ' visit and perambulate ' the commonty ; and if the surveyor's report be not objected to, there will be a decree carrying it into effect.

It is the monotony and the sad sameness of the lot of the poor, as much as their physical wants or painful toiling, that are their curse. They bend their patient necks to the yoke of the severest labour, and in time they take to the roughest fare, and it is their

---

[1] The above quotation is from an article contributed by me to the *Spectator* of December 23, 1871.

safety and comfort that they do so. They bear also
the dull monotony of their daily toil without com-
plaining; but ofttimes this is their ruin, for patience
is here surrender, and often this insidious submissive-
ness, this absence of human unrest, unmans them,
and they come to know no wants only because they
lose all capacity for varied enjoyment. Now, none
'that would wish to chequer and humanize the
lot of the poor would lightly take from them the
commons, which have been their parks, and which
have been the cisterns and sources to them of many
simple and abiding joys. I see a village much like
its fellows in every English county : at the doors of
its modest cottages spreads out a common, bright in
summer with gorse and heath and tremulous blue
bells?; a breezy plain fit for all manly sports; the
one place where the widow may graze her cow ; the
one spot where the poor may glean at all seasons ;
and among the few portions of his country where a
landless Englishman need not feel a trespasser. The
common is doomed. It is broken up and fenced
about. It is trenched and tilled with care. Ten
years hence it is bright with corn, and smiles with

looks of plenty, and those who knew it as an open, barren plain perhaps say, Behold the mighty gain! No gipsies' encampments beside the village; more produce; larger farms; the country more thickly peopled; the poetry and the beauty that dwell in waving corn and scented hayfields—such, it may be said, are the solid fruits of the policy of enclosing. But when all these are counted up, there remains the fact that the village has become a more cheer-less home for the labourer, from many pleasures quite cut off; that his lot is more monotonous and machine-like; and that, denied free access to the open air and room for manly games, he becomes less human, if more civilised—less happy, if more patient—than his father. The new order may be a higher civilisation. But, if so, civilisation has its victims, and perpetrates cruelties of its own; it mutilates and maims, if it does not burn; it en-feebles a community if it destroys no individual; and the dwellers in this village are among the sufferers. A few parks for the people are but an inadequate recompense for such losses. Many com-mons have been turned into parks, and many private parks may be made common before the balance be restored.

There were, moreover, other benefits of a more palpable character, which have been lost. ' Before the commons were parcelled out, there existed potent and well-understood checks on the over-growth of population. Most of the rural poor were then proprietors, not, indeed, of the *directum dominium*, but of a substantial *usus*. This truth is too often forgotten. How rarely is it recollected that it is only in very modern times that England came to be peopled by persons totally devoid of proprietorial rights ! Our present condition is chiefly the work of the eighteenth and nineteenth centuries. Our present artificial state—artificial, whether Lord Derby or Mr. Bright is right as to the number of landowners—is most modern. Long after the destruction of the bulk of our yeo-men, and the diminution of small holdings during the French wars, the mass of the people were to all intents and purposes proprietors. If they did not own the entire *dominium*, neither did the lord of the manor. If they were not the owners of the fee-simple, still they were possessed of some claims over the land.   The pertinent circumstance is, that far into the eighteenth century and into this century England was inhabited by persons who, whether freeholders, or copyholders, or cotters, or residents in towns possessing rights of common, owned proprietorial rights over the soil, and that the present homeless character of the bulk of the people came to pass within living memory.   Even if the labourers were not really occupiers of the soil with fixity of tenure, estover, turbary, pasturage, rights of common appurtenant, appendant, or in gross, were valuable and substantial qualities, and the ownership of some or any of them severed the hind of those days as much from the hind of our day as he is severed from a tiller of the Pays du Waes. In the light of a sound polity, this partnership was often a salutary circumstance.   All the partners had a plain intelligible standard whereby to regulate their lives.   Families must be shaped to fit the land or *usus* at their disposal.   Too many for the land, too many to live.   No part in the agricultural communities, no part in life.   The sequence was direct and most clear. All could understand that pitiless logic. Now, it is a matter of history that countries the population of which has been greatly dependent for sustenance on the soil have been rarely troubled with pauperism, and *a fortiori*, this would hold good of smaller communities the precise means of which were still more visible. But all cannot understand the dependence of wages on capital, an abstraction about the extent and nature of which even experts, not to say the un-initiated, are interminably disputing. Then, too, prudence in such a situation told most speedily and visibly to one's individual benefit. Now, a man's individual hand is palsied by the thought that, labour as he may, the imprudence of others may efface all traces of his forethought. Telling a labourer to contract the size of his family is telling him to swim hard in order that another man, not necessarily he, may reach the shore. If there were then no historical evidence, we should unhesitatingly conclude that a system which indicated in figures the exact number of vacancies or berths could not but be a salutary check on population. Indeed,

Tusser, in his rhymed arguments for enclosures, expressly states that a leading recommendation of enclosures was their tendency to augment population.'[1]

From the preceding sketch, it will be apparent that the manner in which the commons have been divided has been by no means in unison with justice to all concerned or in accordance with their origin. Once, almost every dweller in a manor, unless, indeed, such as were not freemen, had a share in the produce of the common. Perhaps the lord's right always was, until the day of division, of a purely honorary character. Perhaps his legal estate may have been as empty and valueless as the legal estate of a trustee. If he ventured to put up a wall or fence to hinder the commoners' cattle from grazing, it would be cast down. To all intents and purposes, the commoners and not he owned the common. But when a division takes place, those whose rights over the common are of a substantial character may get almost nothing, while those whose

---

[1] The above quotation is from an article contributed by me to the *Spectator* of Dec. 23, 1871.

rights are a figment of law may get almost every-thing. The former are stripped of immemorial en-joyments, and the latter are gifted with powers which were never theirs before ; and the lord's right at Common Law to the shell is converted into a right to the oyster itself.

To what has been done, we must resign our-selves, for ancient wrongs make modern rights. But there are still many commons fit for enclosure and not a little waste land which may one day be culti-vated.[1] The traveller who passes through Matter-dale Common, for instance, beholds a splendid tract of some thousand acres fit for the plough yet lying almost useless. For the enclosure of these com-mons, and such as these, the Statute of Merton, the 6 and 7 Will. iv. c. 115, and the General Enclosure Act, do not afford due facilities. More are required. But let us adopt new principles in regard to enclosures. No man has a vested claim to obtain an Act of Parliament, and without it

---

[1] It has been computed by Captain Maxse that of the waste lands of the United Kingdom, amounting to 27,287,919 acres, 11,000,000 are cultivable.—*Fortnightly Review*, August 1870.

the lord's right may be zero.   If, when an enclosure takes place, he receives an allotment proportioned, not, as now, to the rental or rateable value of his land, but to the actual value of his previous rights over the common, he would be compensated. Such a principle would revolutionise schemes of enclosure, and the lion's share would go to the parish or local community, and not, as now, to the lord.

APPENDIX A

It may be expedient to point out the main characteristics of the system of registration devised by Sir Robert Torrens. His is a system of registration of title as opposed to a registration of assurances. One of the great features of his system is, that he proposes to put on the register all legal interests, such as mortgages, leases, life tenancies, excluding only equitable interests, such as trusts. The other is, that no property will be conveyed by mere execution of a deed or instrument, that instruments will serve only as authorities to make entries, and that conveyance will be accomplished by registration. The former is a point of detail to be tested by experience; the latter is a vital point. I may here mention as proof of the unsatisfactory character of the working of Lord Westbury's Act, that it has been computed that 760 years would, at the present rate, be required in order to put the whole soil of England on the register. See Mr. Arthur Arnold's article on 'Land Transfer' in *Fraser's Magazine* for March 1873.

LONDON : PRINTED BY
SPOTTISWOODE AND CO., NEW-STREET SQUARE
AND PARLIAMENT STREET

www.ingramcontent.com/pod-product-compliance
Lightning Source LLC
Chambersburg PA
CBHW020847270326
41928CB00006B/592